Spanish
Phrasebook

BROCKHAMPTON PRESS
LONDON

This edition published 1995 by Brockhampton Press,
a member of the Hodder Headline PLC Group

ISBN 1 86019 077 4

4 6 8 10 9 7 5 3

Printed and bound in the UK

CONTENTS

CONTENTS

CONTENTS

KEY TO PRONUNCIATION

Guide to Spanish pronunciation scheme

Vowels

a   as in b<u>a</u>d, f<u>a</u>ther
ay   as a in g<u>a</u>te
e   as in b<u>e</u>t
ee   as in s<u>ee</u>
i   as in b<u>i</u>t
o   as in h<u>o</u>t
oo   as in p<u>oo</u>l
u   is pronouned as w
y   as in <u>y</u>acht

Consonants

c   (before e and i) sounds as <u>th</u> in <u>th</u>ank
h   is not pronounced
ñ   sounds as <u>ny</u> in ca<u>ny</u>on
z   sounds as <u>th</u> in <u>th</u>ank

Hyphens are given to show syllables but should be ignored when speaking. The stressed syllable in a word is in bold type.

GETTING STARTED

Everyday words and phrases

Yes
Sí
see

Please
Por favor
por fa-bor

Yes, please
Sí, por favor
see, por fa-bor

Thank you
Gracias
gra-thee-as

No
No
no

Excuse me
¡Perdón!
pair-don

No, thank you
No, gracias
no, gra-thee-as

Good
Bueno
bway-no

OK
Vale
ba-lay

I am very sorry
Lo siento mucho
lo see-en-to moo-cho

Being understood

I do not speak Spanish
No hablo castellano
no a-blo kas-te-ya-no

I do not understand
No entiendo
no en-tyen-do

Being understood

Can you find someone who speaks English?
Puede encontrar a alguien que hable inglés?
pwe-day en-kon-trar al-gee-en kay a-blay een-gles

Can you help me, please?
Puede ayudarme, por favor?
pwe-day a-yoo-dar-may, por fa-bor

It does not matter
No importa
no eem-por-ta

I do not mind
No me importa
no may eem-por-ta

Please repeat that slowly
Por favor repítame eso lentamente
por fa-bor, re-pee-ta-may e-so len-ta-men-tay

Greetings and exchanges

Hello
Hola
o-la

Hi
Hola
o-la

Good evening
Buenas tardes
bway-nas tar-des

Good morning
Buenos días
bway-nos dee-as

Good night
Buenas noches
bway-nas no-ches

Good-bye
Adiós
a-dee-os

Greetings and exchanges

It is nice to meet you
Encantado (encantada) de conocerle
en-kan-ta-do (en-kan-ta-da) day ko-no-thair-lay

How are you?
¿Qué tal estás?
kay tal es-tas

I am very well, thank you
Muy bien, gracias
mwee byen, gra-thee-as

It is good to see you
Me alegro de verlo
may a-le-gro day bair-lo

There are five of us
Somos cinco
so-mos theen-ko

Here is my son
Aquí está mi hijo
a-kee e-sta mee ee-ho

This is — my daughter
Ésta es — mi hija
es-ta es — mee ee-ha

> **— my husband**
> — mi marido
> *— mee ma-ree-do*

> **— my wife**
> — mi esposa
> *— mee es-po-sa*

Greetings and exchanges

My name is...
Me llamo...
may ya-mo...

What is your name?
¿Cómo te llamas?
ko-mo tay ya-mas

I am a student
Soy estudiante
soy es-too-dee-an-tay

I am on holiday
Estoy de vacaciones
es-toy day ba-ka-thyo-nes

I live in London
Vivo en Londres
bee-bo en lon-dres

You are very kind
Es usted muy amable
es oo-sted mwee a-ma-blay

You are very welcome!
¡De nada!
day na-da!

See you soon
Hasta pronto
a-sta pron-to

I am from America
Soy de los Estados Unidos
soy day los es-ta-dos oo-nee-dos

Greetings and exchanges

I am from — Australia
  Soy de — Australia
  *soy day — ow-**stra**-lee-a*

              — Britain
              — Gran Bretaña
              *— gran bre-**ta**-nya*

              — Canada
              — Canadá
              *— ka-na-**da***

              — England
              — Inglaterra
              *— een-gla-**te**-ra*

              — Ireland
              — Irlanda
              *— eer-**lan**-da*

              — New Zealand
              — Nueva Zelanda
              *— **nway**-ba the-**lan**-da*

              — Scotland
              — Escocia
              *— es-**ko**-thee-a*

              — South Africa
              — Sudáfrica
              *— soo-**da**-free-ka*

              — Wales
              — Gales
              *— **ga**-les*

Common questions

Where?
¿Dónde?
don-day

How?
¿Cómo?
ko-mo

Where is...?
¿Dónde está...?
don-day es-ta...

How much?
¿Cuánto?
kwan-to

Where are...?
¿Dónde están...?
don-day es-tan...

Who?
¿Quién?
kee-en

When?
¿Cuándo?
kwan-do

Why?
¿Por qué?
por kay

What?
¿Qué?
kay

Which?
¿Cuál?
kwal

How long will it take?
¿Cuánto tardará?
kwan-to tar-da-ra

How can I contact my American Express / Diners Club?
¿Cómo puedo contactar la oficina de American Express/ Diners club?
ko-mo pwe-do kon-tak-tar la o-fee-thee-na day American Express/Diners Club

Common questions

What is the problem?
¿Cuál es el problema?
kwal es el pro-blay-ma

Do you know a good restaurant
¿Conoce algún buen restaurante?
ko-no-thay al-goon bwen res-to-ran-tay

Do you mind if I...?
¿Le importa que yo...?
lay eem-por-ta kay yo...

What is wrong?
¿Qué ocurre?
kay o-koo-ray

What time do you close?
¿A qué hora cierran?
a kay o-ra thee-e-ran

Where can I buy a postcard?
¿Dónde puedo comprar una postal?
don-day pwe-do kom-prar oo-na po-stal

Where can I buy currency?
¿Dónde puedo cambiar dinero en efectivo?
don-day pwe-do kam-byar dee-ne-ro en e-fek-tee-bo

Where can I change traveller's cheques?
¿Dónde puedo cambiar cheques de viaje?
don-day pwe-do kam-byar che-kays day bee-a-hay

Where can we sit down?
¿Dónde podemos sentarnos?
don-day po-day-mos sen-tar-nos

Common questions

Where is the toilet?
¿Dónde están los servicios?
don-day e-stan los sair-bee-thee-os

Who did this?
¿Quién ha hecho esto?
kee-en a e-cho es-to

Who should I see about this?
¿Con quién debería hablar sobre esto?
kon kee-en de-be-ree-a a-blar so-bray es-to

Will you come also?
¿Va a venir usted también?
ba a be-neer oo-sted tam-byen

What time do you close?
¿A qué hora cierran ?
a kay o-ra thee-e-ran

Asking the time

What time is it?
¿Qué hora es?
kay o-ra es

It is...
Son...
son

a quarter past ten	**a quarter to eleven**
las diez y cuarto	las once menos cuarto
las dee-eth ee kwar-to	*las on-thay me-nos kwar-to*

Asking the time

after three o'clock
después de las tres
des-pwes day las tres

at about one o'clock
hacia la una
a-thee-a la oo-na

at half past six
a las seis y media
a las says ee me-dee-a

twenty five past ten
las diez y veinticinco
las dee-eth ee bain-tee-theen-ko

twenty five to eleven
las once menos veinticinco
las on-thay me-nos bain-tee-theen-ko

at night
por la noche
por la no-chay

early
temprano
tem-pra-no

eleven o'clock
las once
las on-thay

five past ten
las diez y cinco
las dee-eth ee theen-ko

half past ten
las diez y media
las dee-eth ee me-dee-a

twelve o'clock (midday)
las doce (mediodía)
las do-thay (me-dee-o-dee-a)

half past eight exactly
a las ocho y media en punto
a las o-cho ee me-dee-a en poon-to

five to eleven
las once menos cinco
las on-thay me-nos theen-ko

in an hour's time
dentro de una hora
den-tro day oo-na o-ra

in half an hour
dentro de media hora
den-tro day me-dee-a o-ra

late
tarde
tar-day

Asking the time

before midnight
antes de medianoche
an-tes day me-dee-a-no-chay

this afternoon
esta tarde
es-ta tar-day

midnight
medianoche
me-dee-a-no-chay

this evening
esta tarde
es-ta tar-day

nearly five o'clock
casi las cinco
ka-see las theen-ko

this morning
por la mañana
por la man-ya-na

soon
pronto
pron-to

tonight
esta noche
es-ta no-chay

ten o' clock
las diez
las dee-eth

twenty past ten
las diez y veinte
las dee-eth ee bain-tay

ten past ten
las diez y diez
las dee-eth ee dee-eth

twenty to eleven
las once menos veinte
las on-thay me-nos bain-tay

ten to eleven
las once menos diez
las on-thay me-nos dee-eth

two hours ago
hace dos horas
a-thay dos o-ras

Common problems

I am late
Voy con retraso
boy kon re-tra-so

I cannot find my driving licence
No encuentro el permiso de conducir
no en-kwen-tro el per-mee-so day kon-doo-theer

I have dropped a contact lens
Se me ha caído una lentilla
say may a ky-ee-do oo-na len-tee-ya

   I have lost — my credit cards
   He perdido — las tarjetas de crédito
ay pair-dee-do — las tar-hay-tas day kre-dee-to

         — my key
         — la llave
         — la ya-bay

         — my traveller's cheques
         — los cheques de viaje
         — los che-kays day bee-a-hay

I have no currency
No tengo efectivo
no ten-go e-fek-tee-bo

I must see a lawyer
Tengo que hablar con un abogado
ten-go kay a-blar kon oon a-bo-ga-do

Common problems

My car has been stolen
Me han robado el coche
may an ro-ba-do el ko-chay

My handbag has been stolen
Me han robado el bolso
may an ro-ba-do el bol-so

My wallet has been stolen
Me han robado la cartera
may an ro-ba-do la kar-tair-ra

AT THE AIRPORT

Arrival

Here is my passport
Aquí está mi pasaporte
a-kee e-sta mee pa-sa-por-tay

How long will this take?
¿Cuánto tardará esto?
kwan-to tar-da-ra es-to

I am attending a convention
Voy a asistir a un congreso
boy a a-see-steer a oon kon-gre-so

I am here on business
Estoy aquí en viaje de negocios
es-toy a-kee en bee-a-hay day ne-go-thee-os

I will be staying here for eight weeks
Me quedaré aquí ocho semanas
may kay-da-ray a-kee o-cho se-ma-nas

We are visiting friends
Estamos visitando a amigos
es-ta-mos bee-see-tan-do a-mee-gos

We have a joint passport
Tenemos un pasaporte familiar
te-nay-mos oon pa-sa-por-tay fa-mee-lyar

How much do I have to pay?
¿Cuánto tengo que pagar?
kwan-to ten-go kay pa-gar

Arrival

I have nothing to declare
No tengo nada que declarar
no ten-go na-da kay de-kla-rar

I have the usual allowances
Tengo los artículos permitidos
ten-go los ar-tee-koo-los pair-mee-tee-dos

This is for my own use
Esto es para mi uso personal
es-to es pa-ra mee oo-so pair-so-nal

Common problems and requests

Can I upgrade to first class?
¿Puedo cambiar mi billete a primera clase?
pway-do kam-byar mee bee-ye-tay a pree-me-ra kla-say

I have lost my ticket
He perdido el billete
ay pair-dee-do el bee-ye-tay

I have missed my connection
He perdido el vuelo de enlace
ay pair-dee-do el bway-lo day en-la-thay

Please give me back my passport
Devuélvame el pasaporte, por favor
de-bwel-ba-may el pa-sa-por-tay, por fa-bor

The people who were to meet me have not arrived
No ha llegado la gente que iba a recibirme
no a ye-ga-do la hen-tay kay ee-ba a re-thee-beer-may

Common problems and requests

Where can I find the airline representative?
¿Dónde puedo encontrar al representante de la compañía
aérea?
*don-day pwe-do en-kon-trar al re-pre-zen-tan-tay day la
kom-pa-nyee-a a-air-ay-a*

Where do I get the connection flight to Santiago?
¿Dónde puedo enlazar con el vuelo a Santiago?
don-day pwe-do en-la-thar kon el bway-lo a san-tee-a-go

   Where is — the bar?
 ¿Dónde está — el bar?
don-day es-ta — el bar

      — the toilet?
      — los servicios?
      — los sair-bee-thee-os

      — the departure lounge?
      — la sala de embarque?
      — la sa-la day em-bar-kay

      — the information desk?
      — la oficina de información?
      — la o-fee-thee-na day een-for-ma-thyon

      — the transfer desk?
      — el mostrador de transbordos?
      — el mos-tra-dor day trans-bor-dos

Is there a bus into town?
¿Hay autobús a la ciudad?
a-ee ow-to-boos a la thee-oo-dad

Common problems and requests

How long will the delay be?
¿Cuánto se retrasará?
kwan-to say re-tra-sa-ra

I was delayed at the airport
Me entretuvieron en el aeropuerto
may en-tray-too-byair-ron en el a-air-o-pwair-to

My flight was late
Mi vuelo se retrasó
mee bway-lo say re-tra-so

I was held up at immigration
Me entretuvieron en el control de pasaportes
may en-tray-too-byair-ron en el kon-trol day pa-sa-por-tes

Luggage

Where is the baggage from flight number...?
¿Dónde están los equipajes del vuelo número...?
don-day es-tan los e-kee-pa-hays del bway-lo noo-me-ro...

I have lost my bag
He perdido la bolsa
ay pair-dee-do la bol-sa

These bags are not mine
Estas bolsas no son mías
es-tas bol-sas no son mee-as

Are there any baggage trolleys?
¿Hay carritos de equipaje?
a-ee ka-ree-tos day e-kee-pa-hay

Luggage

Can I have help with my bags
¿Puedo obtener ayuda para llevar el equipaje?
pwe-do ob-te-nair a-yoo-da pa-ra ye-bar el e-kee-pa-hay

Is there any charge?
¿Hay que pagar algo?
a-ee kay pa-gar al-go

I will carry that myself
Esto lo llevaré yo mismo (misma)
es-to lo ye-ba-ray yo miz-mo

My baggage has not arrived
No ha llegado mi equipaje
no a ye-ga-do mee e-kee-pa-hay

Where is my bag?
¿Dónde está mi bolsa?
don-day es-ta mee bol-sa

It is — a large suitcase
　　　— una maleta grande
　　　— oo ma-lay-ta gran-day

　　　— a rucksack
　　　— una mochila
　　　— oo-na mo-chee-la

　　　— a small bag
　　　— una bolsa pequeña
　　　— oo-na bol-sa pe-ken-ya

No, do not put that on top
No, no ponga eso encima de todo
no, no pon-ga e-so en-thee-ma day to-do

Luggage

Please take these bags to a taxi
Por favor lleve estas bolsas a un taxi
por fa-bor, ye-bay es-tas bol-sas a oon tak-see

Careful, the handle is broken
Cuidado, el mango está roto
kwee-da-do, el man-go es-ta ro-to

This package is fragile
Este paquete es frágil
es-tay pa-ke-tay es fra-heel

AT THE HOTEL

Reservations and enquiries

I am sorry I am late
Siento llegar tarde
*syen-to ye-**gar tar**-day*

I have a reservation
Tengo una reserva hecha
ten-go oo-na re-sair-ba ay-cha

I shall be staying until July 4th
Me quedaré hasta el cuatro de julio
*may ke-da-**ray** a-sta el **kwa**-tro day **hoo**-lee-o*

I want to stay for 5 nights
Quiero quedarme cinco noches
*kee-e-ro ke-**dar**-may **theen**-ko **no**-ches*

Do you have a double room with a bath?
¿Tiene una habitación doble con baño?
*tee-e-nay oo-na a-bee-ta-**thyon** do-blay kon **ban**-yo*

Do you have a room with twin beds and a shower?
¿Tiene una habitación con camas gemelas y ducha?
*tee-e-nay oo-na a-bee-ta-**thyon** kon **ka**-mas he-**may**-las ee **doo**-cha*

Do you have a single room?
¿Tiene una habitación individual?
*tee-e-nay oo-na a-bee-ta-**thyon** een-dee-bee-**dwal***

Reservations and enquiries

     I need — a double room with a bed for a child
Necesito — una habitación doble con una cama para
          un niño
ne-the-see-to— oo-na a-bee-ta-thyon do-blay kon oo-na ka-
         ma pa-ra oon neen-yo

        — a room with a double bed
        — una habitación con cama doble
        — oo-na a-bee-ta-thyon kon ka-ma do-blay

        — a room with twin beds and bath
        — una habitación con camas gemelas y baño
        — oo-na a-bee-ta-thyon kon ka-mas he-may-
        las ee ban-yo

        — a single room
        — una habitación individual
        — oo-na a-bee-ta-thyon een-dee-bee-dwal

        — a single room with a shower or bath
        — una habitación individual con ducha o baño
        — oo-na a-bee-ta-thyon een-dee-bee-dwal kon
        doo-cha o ban-yo

How much is — full board?
  ¿Cuánto es — la pensión completa?
  kwan-to es — la pen-syon kom-play-ta

        — half-board?
        — la media pensión?
        — la me-dee-a pen-syon

How much is it per night?
¿Cuánto cuesta por noche?
kwan-to kwes-ta por no-chay

Reservations and enquiries

Does the price include — room and breakfast?
¿Están incluidos en el precio — la habitación y el
                                                 desayuno?
es-tan een-kloo-ee-dos en el — la a-bee-ta-thyon ee el
         pre-thee-o   des-a-yoo-no

— room and all meals?
— ¿la habitación y todas las comidas?
— *la a-bee-ta-thyon ee to-das las ko-mee-das*

— room and dinner?
— ¿la habitación y la cena?
— *la a-bee-ta-thyon ee la thay-na*

Can we have adjoining rooms?
¿Nos puede dar habitaciones contiguas?
nos pwe-day dar a-bee-ta-thyo-nes kon-tee-gwas

Are there other children staying at the hotel?
¿Hay más niños hospedados en el hotel?
a-ee mas neen-yos os-pe-da-dos en el o-tel

Are there supervised activities for the children?
¿Hay actividades vigiladas para los niños?
a-ee ak-tee-bee-da-des bee-hee-la-das pa-ra los neen-yos

Can my son sleep in our room?
¿Puede dormir mi hijo en nuestra habitación?
pwe-day dor-meer mee ee-ho en nwes-tra a-bee-ta-thyon

Do you take traveller's cheques?
¿Acepta cheques de viaje?
a-thep-ta che-kays day bee-a-hay

Reservations and enquiries

Which floor is my room on?
¿En qué piso está mi habitación?
*en kay **pee**-so es-**ta** mee a-bee-ta-**thyon***

Do you have a fax machine?
¿Tiene fax?
tee-e-nay faks

Do you have a laundry service?
¿Tienen servicio de lavandería?
*tee-e-nen sair-**bee**-thee-o day la-ban-de-**ree**-a*

Do you have a safe for valuables?
¿Tiene caja fuerte para objetos de valor?
*tee-e-nay **ka**-ha **fwair**-tay **pa**-ra ob-**he**-tos day ba-**lor***

Do you have any English newspapers?
¿Tiene periódicos en inglés?
*tee-e-nay pe-ree-o-dee-kos en een-**gles***

Do you have a car park?
¿Tienen aparcamiento?
*tee-e-nen a-par-ka-**myen**-to*

Do you have a cot for my baby?
¿Tiene una cuna para el bebé?
*tee-e-nay **oo**-na **coo**-na **pa**-ra el be-**bay***

Do you have satellite TV?
¿Tiene antena parabólica?
*tee-e-nay an-**tay**-na pa-ra-**bo**-lee-ka*

What is the voltage here?
¿Qué voltaje hay aquí?
*kay bol-**ta**-hay **a**-ee a-**kee***

Reservations and enquiries

Is there — a casino?
  ¿Hay — casino?
  a-ee — ka-see-no

    — a hairdryer?
    — secador de pelo?
    *— se-ka-**dor** day **pay**-lo*

    — a lift?
    — ascensor?
    *— as-then-**sor***

    — a minibar?
    — minibar?
    *— mee-nee-**bar***

    — a sauna?
    — sauna?
    *— **sow**-na*

    — a swimming pool?
    — piscina?
    *— pees-**thee**-na*

    — a telephone?
    — teléfono?
    *— te-**le**-fo-no*

    — a television?
    — televisión?
    *— te-lay-bee-**syon***

    — a trouser press?
    — plancha para pantalones?
    *— **plan**-cha **pa**-ra pan-ta-**lo**-nes*

Reservations and enquiries

Is there a room service menu?
¿Hay menú para el servicio de habitaciones?
a-ee me-noo pa-ra el sair-bee-thee-o day a-bee-ta-thyo-nes

Is there a market in the town?
¿Hay algún mercado en la ciudad?
a-ee al-goon mair-ka-do en la thee-oo-dad

Is there a Chinese restaurant?
¿Hay algún restaurante chino?
a-ee al-goon re-sto-ran-tay chee-no

Is there an Indian restaurant?
¿Hay algún restaurante indio?
a-ee al-goon re-sto-ran-tay een-dee-o

Is this a safe area?
¿Es esta una zona segura?
es es-ta oo-na tho-na se-goo-ra

Where is the socket for my razor?
¿Dónde está el enchufe de la máquina de afeitar?
don-day es-ta el en-choo-fay day la ma-kee-nee-ya day a-fay-tar

Is the voltage 220 or 110?
¿Es el voltaje de doscientos veinte o de ciento diez?
es el bol-ta-hay day dos-thee-en-tos bain-tay o day thee-en-to dee-eth

What time does the hotel close?
¿A qué hora cierra el hotel?
a kay o-ra thee-e-ra el o-tel

Service

What time does the restaurant close?
¿A qué hora cierra el restaurante?
a kay o-ra thee-e-ra el re-sto-ran-tay

When does the bar open?
¿Cuándo se abre el bar?
kwan-do say a-bray el bar

  What time is — breakfast?
¿Á qué hora es — el desayuno?
  a kay o-ra es — el des-a-yoo-no

                          — dinner?
                          — la cena
                          — la thay-na

                          — lunch?
                          — la comida?
                          — la ko-mee-da

Service

Can I charge this to my room?
¿Puede cargar esto a mi cuenta?
pwe-day kar-gar es-to a mee kwen-ta

Can I dial direct from my room?
¿Puedo marcar directamente desde mi habitación?
pwe-do mar-kar dee-rek-ta-men-tay dez-day mee a-bee-ta-thyon

Can I have a newspaper?
¿Me da un periódico?
may da oon pe-ree-o-dee-ko

Service

Can I have an outside line?
¿Me da línea, por favor?
*may da **lee**-nay-a, por fa-**bor***

Can I have my wallet from the safe?
¿Puedo sacar mi cartera de la caja fuerte?
*pwe-do sa-**kar** mee kar-**tair**-a day la **ka**-ha fwair-tay, por fa-**bor***

Can I have the bill please
¿Puede darme la factura, por favor?
*pwe-day **dar**-may la fak-**too**-ra, por fa-**bor***

Can I hire a portable telephone?
¿Puedo alquilar un teléfono portátil?
*pwe-do al-kee-**lar** oon te-**le**-fo-no por-**ta**-teel*

Can I make a telephone call from here?
¿Puedo hacer una llamada telefónica desde aquí?
*pwe-do a-**thair** oo-na ya-**ma**-da te-le-fo-**nee**-ka **dez**-day a-**kee***

Can I send this by courier?
¿Puedo enviar esto por mensajero?
*pwe-do en-**byar** es-to por men-sa-**hair**-o*

Can I use my charge card?
¿Puedo utilizar mi tarjeta de pago?
*pwe-do oo-tee-lee-**thar** mee tar-**hay**-ta day **pa**-go*

Can I use my personal computer here?
¿Puedo utilizar aquí mi ordenador personal?
*pwe-do oo-tee-lee-**thar** a-**kee** mee or-de-na-**dor** pair-so-**nal***

Can I use traveller's cheques?
¿Puedo utilizar cheques de viaje?
*pwe-do oo-tee-lee-**thar** che-kays day bee-a-**hay***

Service

Can we have breakfast in our room, please?
¿Podemos desayunar en la habitación , por favor?
*po-**day**-mos des-a-yoo-**nar** en la a-bee-ta-**thyon**, por fa-**bor***

Can you recommend a good local restaurant?
¿Puede recomendar un buen restaurante cercano?
*pwe-**day** re-ko-men-**dar** oon bwen re-sto-**ran**-tay thair-**ka**-no*

I want to stay an extra night
Quiero quedarme una noche más
*kee-e-ro ke-**dar**-may oo-na **no**-chay mas*

Do I have to change rooms?
¿Tengo que cambiarme de habitación?
ten**-go kay kam-**byar** may day a-bee-ta-**thyon

I need an early morning call
Necesito que me llame por la mañana temprano
*ne-the-**see**-to kay may **ya**-may por la man-**ya**-na tem-**pra**-no*

       I need — a razor
      Necesito — una maquinilla de afeitar
*ne-the-**see**-to — oo-na ma-kee-**nee**-ya day a-fay-**tar***

             — some soap
             — jabón
             *— ha-**bon***

             — some toilet paper
             — papel higiénico
             *— pa-**pel** ee-**hyen**-ee-ko*

             — some towels
             — toallas
             *— to-**a**-yas*

Service

I need to charge these batteries
Tengo que cargar estas pilas
ten-go kay kar-gar es-tas pee-las

I want to press these clothes
Quiero planchar esta ropa
kee-e-ro plan-char es-ta ro-pa

Is there a trouser press I can use?
¿Hay prensa para pantalones que pueda usar?
a-ee pren-sa pa-ra pan-ta-lo-nes kay pwe-do oo-sar

Please fill the minibar
Por favor, llene el minibar
por fa-bor, ye-nay el mee-nee-bar

Please leave the bags in the lobby
Por favor, deje las bolsas en el vestíbulo
por fa-bor, de-hay las bol-sas en el bes-tee-boo-lo

Please send this fax for me
Por favor, envie este fax de mi parte
por fa-bor, en-bee-ay es-tay faks day mee par-tay

Please turn the heating off
Apague la calefacción, por favor
a-pa-gay la ka-le-fak-thyon, por fa-bor

Please, wake me at 7 o'clock in the morning
Por favor, llámeme a las siete de la mañana
por fa-bor, ya-may-may a las see-e-tay day la man-ya-na

Where can I send a fax?
¿Dónde puedo enviar un fax?
don-day pwe-do en-byar oon faks

Service

Can I have — my key, please?
¿Puede darme — mi llave, por favor?
pwe-day dar-may — mee ya-bay, por fa-bor

— an ashtray?
— un cenicero?
— oon the-nee-thair-o

— another blanket?
— otra manta?
— o-tra man-ta

— another pillow?
— otra almohada?
— o-tra al-mo-a-da

— some coat hangers?
— algunas perchas?
— al-goo-nas pair-chas

— some notepaper?
— papel de cartas?
— pa-pel day kar-tas

Has my colleague arrived yet?
¿Ha llegado mi compañero?
a ye-ga-do mee kom-pan-ye-ro

I am expecting a fax
Estoy esperando un fax
es-toy es-pe-ran-do oon faks

My room number is 22
El número de mi habitación es el veintidós
el noo-me-ro day mee a-bee-ta-thyon es el bain-tee-dos

Service

Please can I leave a message?
¿Puedo dejar un mensaje, por favor?
pwe-do de-har oon men-sa-hay, por fa-bor

Problems

Where is the manager?
¿Dónde está el gerente?
don-day es-ta el he-ren-tay

I cannot close the window
No puedo cerrar la ventana
no pwe-do the-rar la ben-ta-na

I cannot open the window
No puedo abrir la ventana
no pwe-do a-breer la ben-ta-na

The air conditioning is not working
No funciona el aire acondicionado
no foon-thyo-na el a-ee-ray a-kon-dee-thyo-na-do

The room key does not work
No funciona la llave de la habitación
no foon-thyo-na la ya-bay day la a-bee-ta-thyon

The bathroom is dirty
El cuarto de baño está sucio
el kwar-to day ban-yo es-ta soo-thyo

The heating is not working
No funciona la calefacción
no foon-thyo-na la ka-le-fak-thyon

The light is not working
No funciona la luz
no foon-thyo-na la looth

The room is not serviced
La habitación no está preparada
la a-bee-ta-thyon no es-ta pre-pa-ra-da

The room is too noisy
La habitación es demasiado ruidosa
la a-bee-ta-thyon es de-ma-sya-do roo-ee-do-so

There are no towels in the room
No hay toallas en la habitación
no a-ee to-a-yas en la a-bee-ta-thyon

There is no hot water
No hay agua caliente
no a-ee a-gwa ka-lee-en-tay

There is no plug for the washbasin
No hay tapón en el lavabo
no a-ee ta-pon en el la-ba-bo

Checking out

I have to leave tomorrow
Tengo que irme mañana
ten-go kay eer-may man-ya-na

We will be leaving early tomorrow
Nos iremos mañana temprano
nos ee-ray-mos man-ya-na tem-pra-no

Checking out

Could you have my bags brought down?
¿Podría hacer que me bajen las bolsas?
po-dree-a a-thair kay may ba-hen las bol-sas

Could you order me a taxi?
¿Puede pedirme un taxi?
pwe-day pe-deer-may oon tak-see

Thank you, we enjoyed our stay
Gracias, hemos disfrutado de nuestra estancia
gra-thee-as, ay-mos dees-froo-ta-do day nwes-tra e-stan-thee-a

OTHER ACCOMODATION

Renting a house

We have rented this villa
Hemos alquilado este chalé
ay-mos al-kee-la-do es-tay cha-lay

Here is our booking form
Aquí tiene nuestra reserva
a-kee tee-e-nay nwes-tra re-sair-ba

We need two sets of keys
Necesitamos dos juegos de llaves
ne-the-see-ta-mos dos hway-gos day ya-bes

Can I contact you on this number?
¿Puedo contactarle en este teléfono?
pwe-do kon-tak-tar-lay en es-tay te-le-fo-no

Where is the bathroom?
¿Dónde está el baño?
don-day es-ta el ban-yo

How does this work?
¿Cómo funciona ésto?
ko-mo foon-thyo-na es-to

I cannot open the shutters
No puedo abrir los postigos
no pwe-do a-breer los po-stee-gos

Can you send a repairman?
¿Puede enviar alguien a reparar?
pwe-day en-byar al-gee-en a re-pa-rar

Renting a house

Is the water heater working?
¿Funciona el calentador de agua?
foon-thyo-na el ka-len-ta-dor day a-gwa

Is the water safe to drink?
¿El agua es potable?
el a-gwa es po-ta-blay

Is there any spare bedding?
¿Hay ropa de cama de más?
a-ee ro-pa day ka-ma day mas

The cooker does not work
No funciona la cocina
no foon-thyo-na la ko-thee-na

The refrigerator does not work
No funciona el frigorífico
no foon-thyo-na el free-go-ree-fee-ko

The toilet is blocked
El inodoro está atascado
el een-o-do-ro es-ta a-ta-ska-do

There is a leak
Hay un escape
a-ee oon es-ka-pay

We do not have any water
No tenemos agua
no te-nay-mos a-gwa

When does the cleaner come?
¿Cuándo vienen a limpiar?
kwan-do bee-e-nen a leem-pyar

Around the house

Where is the fuse box?
¿Dónde están los plomos?
don-day es-tan los plo-mos

Where is the key for this door?
¿Dónde está la llave de esta puerta?
don-day es-ta la ya-bay day es-ta pwair-ta

Around the house

bath
baño
ban-yo

bathroom
cuarto de baño
kwar-to day ban-yo

bed
cama
ka-ma

brush
cepillo
the-pee-yo

can opener
abrelatas
a-bray-la-tas

chair
silla
see-ya

cooker
cocina
ko-thee-na

corkscrew
sacacorchos
sa-ka-kor-chos

cup
taza
ta-tha

fork
tenedor
te-ne-dor

glass
vaso
ba-so

kitchen
cocina
ko-thee-na

Around the house

knife
cuchillo
koo-chee-yo

spoon
cuchara
coo-cha-ra

mirror
espejo
es-pe-ho

stove
estufa
es-too-fa

pan
sartén
sar-ten

table
mesa
may-sa

plate
plato
pla-to

tap
grifo
gree-fo

refrigerator
frigorífico
free-go-ree-fee-ko

toilet
inodoro
een-o-do-ro

sheet
sábana
sa-ba-na

vacuum cleaner
aspirador
as-pee-ra-dor

sink
fregadero
fre-ga-dair-o

washbasin
lavabo
la-ba-bo

Camping

Can we camp in your field?
¿Podemos acampar en su terreno?
*po-**day**-mos a-kam-**par** en soo te-**ray**-no*

Can we camp near here?
¿Podemos acampar cerca de aquí?
*po-**day**-mos a-kam-**par thair**-ka day a-**kee***

Please can we pitch our tent here?
¿Podríamos montar la tienda aquí?
*po-**dree**-a-mos mon-**tar** la tee-**en**-da a-**kee***

Can we park our caravan here?
¿Podemos aparcar la caravana aquí?
*po-**day**-mos a-par-**kar** la ka-ra-**ba**-na a-**kee***

Do I pay in advance?
¿Tengo que pagar de antemano?
*ten-go kay pa-**gar** day an-tay-**ma**-no*

Do I pay when I leave?
¿Tengo que pagar al salir?
*ten-go kay pa-**gar** al sa-**leer***

Is there a more sheltered site?
¿Hay algún lugar más resguardado?
*a-ee al-**goon** loo-**gar** mas res-gwar-**da**-do*

Is there a restaurant or a shop on the site?
¿Hay alguna tienda o restaurante en el camping?
*a-ee al-**goo**-na tee-**en**-da o re-sto-**ran**-tay en el **kam**-peen*

Camping

Is there another campsite near there?
¿Hay algún otro camping cercano?
a-ee al-goon o-tro kam-peen thair-ka-no

Is this the drinking water?
¿Es ésta el agua potable?
es es-ta a-gwa po-ta-blay

The site is very wet and muddy
El terreno está muy húmedo y lleno de barro
el te-ray-no es-ta mwee oo-me-do ee ye-no day ba-ro

Where are the toilets?
¿Dónde están los servicios?
don-day es-tan los sair-bee-thee-os

Where can I have a shower?
¿Dónde puedo ducharme?
don-day pwe-do doo-char-may

Where can we wash our dishes?
¿Dónde podemos fregar los platos?
don-day po-day-mos fre-gar los pla-tos

Around the campsite

Air mattress
Colchoneta hinchable
kol-cho-nay-ta een-cha-blay

bottle-opener
abrebotellas
a-bray-bo-te-yas

backpack
mochila
mo-chee-la

bucket
balde
bal-day

Around the campsite

camp bed
cama plegable
ka-ma ple-ga-blay

camp chair
silla plegable
see-ya ple-ga-blay

can-opener
abrelatas
a-bray-la-tas

candle
vela
bay-la

cup
taza
ta-tha

fire
fuego
fway-go

flashlight
linterna
leen-tair-na

fly sheet
toldo impermeable
tol-do eem-pair-may-a-blay

folding table
mesa plegable
may-sa ple-ga-blay

fork
tenedor
te-ne-dor

frying pan
sartén
sar-ten

ground sheet
suelo impermeable
sway-lo eem-pair-may-a-blay

ground
suelo
sway-lo

guy line
viento
bee-en-to

knife
cuchillo
koo-chee-yo

mallet
mazo
ma-tho

matches
cerillas
thair-ee-yas

pail
cubo
koo-bo

Around the campsite

penknife
navaja
*na-**ba**-ha*

stove
hornilla
*or-**nee**-ya*

plate
plato
***pla**-to*

tent peg
clavija
*kla-**bee**-ha*

rucksack
mochila
*mo-**chee**-la*

tent pole
mástil de tienda
*ma-**steel** day tee-**en**-da*

shelter
refugio
*re-foo-**hyo***

tent
tienda
*tee-**en**-da*

sleeping bag
saco de dormir
*sa-ko day dor-**meer***

thermos flask
termo
***tair**-mo*

spoon
cuchara
koo-cha-ra

torch
linterna
*leen-**tair**-na*

Hostelling

Is there a youth hostel near here?
¿Hay algún albergue juvenil cercano?
*a-ee al-**goon** al-**bair**-gay hoo-be-**neel** thair-**ka**-no*

Can we stay here five nights
¿Podemos quedarnos aquí cinco noches?
*po-**day**-mos ke-**dar**-nos a-**kee theen**-ko **no**-ches*

Hostel   *ling*

Can we stay until Sunday?
¿Podemos quedarnos hasta el domingo?
po-day-mos ke-dar-nos a-sta el do-meen-go

Here is my membership card
Aquí está mi tarjeta de socio
a-kee es-ta mee tar-hay-ta day so-thee-o

I do not have my card
No tengo mi tarjeta
no ten-go mee tar-hay-ta

Can I join here?
¿Puedo hacerme socio aquí?
pwe-do a-thair-may so-thee-o a-kee

Are you open during the day?
¿Está esto abierto durante el día?
es-ta a-bee-air-to doo-ran-tay el dee-a

Can I use the kitchen?
¿Puedo utilizar la cocina?
pwe-do oo-tee-lee-thar la ko-thee-na

What time do you close?
¿A qué hora cierran?
a kay o-ra thee-e-ran

Do you serve meals?
¿Sirven comidas?
seer-ben ko-mee-das

— to take away?
— para llevar?
— pa-ra ye-bar

Childcare

Can you warm this milk for me?
¿Puede calentarme esta leche?
pwe-day ka-len-tar-may es-ta le-chay

Do you have a high chair?
¿Tiene alguna silla alta?
tee-e-nay al-goo-na see-ya al-ta

Is there a baby-sitter?
¿Hay una canguro?
a-ee oo-na kan-goo-ro

Is there a cot for our baby?
¿Hay alguna cuna para nuestro bebé?
a-ee al-goo-na coo-na pa-ra nwes-tra be-bay

Is there a paddling pool?
¿Hay piscina para niños?
a-ee pees-thee-na pa-ra neen-yos

Is there a swimming pool?
¿Hay piscina?
a-ee pees-thee-na

Is there a swing park?
¿Hay parque de columpios?
a-ee par-kay day ko-loom-pyos

I am very sorry. That was very naughty of him
Lo siento mucho. Ha sido una travesura suya
lo see-en-to moo-cho. A see-do oo-na tra-be-soo-ra soo-ya

Childcare

It will not happen again
No volverá a ocurrir
no bol-bair-a a o-koo-reer

How old is your daughter?
¿Cuántos años tiene su hija?
kwan-tos an-yos tee-e-nay soo ee-ha

My daughter is 7 years old
Mi hija tiene siete años
mee ee-ha tee-e-nay see-e-tay an-yos

My son is 10 years old
Mi hijo tiene diez años
mee ee-ho tee-e-nay dee-eth an-yos

She goes to bed at nine o'clock
Se acuesta a las nueve
say a-kwe-sta a las nwe-bay

We will be back in two hours
Volveremos dentro de dos horas
bol-bair-ay-mos den-tro day dos o-ras

Where can I buy some disposable nappies?
¿Dónde puedo comprar pañales desechables?
don-day pwe-do kom-prar pan-ya-les des-e-cha-bles

Where can I change the baby?
¿Dónde puedo cambiar al bebé?
don-day pwe-do kam-byar al be-bay

Where can I feed my baby?
¿Dónde puedo dar de comer al bebé?
don-day pwe-do dar day ko-mair al be-bay

GETTING AROUND

Asking for directions

Where is — the art gallery?
¿Dónde está — el museo de arte?
don-day es-ta — el moo-say-o day ar-tay

— the post office?
— correos?
— ko-ray-os

— the Tourist Information Service?
— la Oficina de Turismo?
— la o-fee-thee-na day too-reez-mo

Can you tell me the way to the bus station?
¿Puede indicarme el camino a la estación de autobuses?
pwe-day een-dee-kar-may el ka-mee-no a la e-sta-thyon day ow-to-boo-ses

I am lost
Estoy perdido/perdida
es-toy pair-dee-do/pair-dee-da

I am lost. How do I get to the Carlos Quinto Hotel?
Estoy perdido (perdida). ¿Cómo se llega al Hotel Carlos Quinto?
es-toy pair-dee-do (pair-dee-da). Ko-mo say ye-ga al o-tel Kar-los Keen-to

Can you show me on the map?
¿Puede indicarme en el mapa?
pwe-day een-dee-kar-may en el ma-pa

Asking for directions

May I borrow your map?
¿Puede prestarme el mapa?
pwe-day pre-star-may el ma-pa

We are looking for a restaurant
Estamos buscando un restaurante
es-ta-mos boo-skan-do oon re-sto-ran-tay

Where are the toilets?
¿Dónde están los servicios?
don-day es-tan los sair-bee-thee-os

I am looking for the Tourist Information Office
Estoy buscando la Oficina de Turismo
es-toy boo-skan-do la o-fee-thee-na day too-reez-mo

I am trying to get to the market
Quiero ir al mercado
kee-e-ro eer al mair-ka-do

Can you walk there?
¿Se puede ir andando hasta allí?
say pwe-day eer an-dan-do a-sta a-yee

Is it far?
¿Está lejos?
es-ta lay-hos

I want to go to the theatre
Quiero ir al teatro
kee-e-ro eer al tay-a-tro

Is there a bus that goes there?
¿Hay algún autobús que vaya allí?
a-ee al-goon ow-to-boos kay ba-ya a-yee

Asking for directions

Where do I get a bus for the city centre?
¿Dónde puedo coger el autobús al centro de la ciudad?
don-day pwe-do ko-hair el ow-to-boos al then-tro day la thee-oo-dad

Is there a train that goes there?
¿Hay algún tren que vaya allí?
a-ee al-goon tren kay ba-ya a-yee

By road

Where does this road go to?
¿Adónde va esta carretera?
a-don-day ba es-ta ka-re-tair-a

Do I turn here for Jaca?
¿Tengo que girar aquí para Jaca?
ten-go kay hee-rar a-kee pa-ra ha-ka

How do I get onto the motorway (highway)?
¿Por dónde se entra a la autopista?
por don-day say en-tra a la ow-to-pee-sta

How far is it to Toledo?
¿Qué distancia hay a Toledo?
kay dee-stan-thee-a a-ee a to-lay-do

How long will it take to get there?
¿Cuánto se tarda en ir allí?
kwan-to say tar-da en eer a-yee

I am looking for the next exit
Busco la siguiente salida
boos-ko la see-gee-en-tay sa-lee-da

Directions

Is there a filling station near here?
¿Hay una gasolinera aquí cerca?
a-ee oo-na ga-so-lee-nair-a a-kee thair-ka

Is this the right way to the supermarket?
¿Es éste el camino al supermercado?
es es-tay el ka-mee-no al soo-pair-mair-ka-do

Which is the best route to Pamplona?
¿Cuál es la mejor carretera para Pamplona?
kwal es la me-hor ka-re-tair-a pa-ra Pam-plo-na

Which is the fastest route?
¿Cuál es la carretera más rapida?
kwal es la ka-re-tair-a mas ra-pee-da

Which road do I take to Segovia?
¿Qué carretera debo coger para Segovia?
kay ka-re-tair-a de-bo ko-hair pa-ra se-go-bee-a

Directions

You go — as far as...
   Vaya — hasta...
   by-a — a-sta

> **— left**
> — a la izquierda
> *— a la eeth-kyair-da*

> **— right**
> — a la derecha
> *— a la de-ray-cha*

Directions

You go towards...
Vaya hacia...
by-a-thya a-thya

It is — at the intersection
Está — en el cruce
es-ta — en el croo-thay

    — around the corner
    — a la vuelta de la esquina
    — a la bwel-ta day la es-kee-na

    — under the bridge
    — bajo el puente
    — ba-ho el pwen-tay

    — after the traffic lights
    — después del semáforo
    — des-pwes del se-ma-fo-ro

    — next to the cinema
    — junto al cine
    — hoon-to al thee-nay

    — on the next floor
    — en el siguiente piso
    — en el see-gee-en-tay pee-so

    — opposite the railway station
    — frente a la estación de ferrocarril
    — fren-tay a la es-ta-thyon day fe-ro-ka-reel

    — over there
    — allí
    — a-yee

Directions

Cross the street
Atraviese la calle
a-tra-bee-ay-say la ka-yay

Follow the signs for...
Siga las señales a...
see-ga las sen-ya-les a...

— the next junction
— el próximo cruce
— el prok-see-mo croo-thay

— the motorway
— la autopista
— la ow-to-pee-sta

— the square
— la plaza
— la pla-tha

Keep going straight ahead
Siga todo recto
see-ga to-do rek-to

Turn left
gire a la izquierda
hee-ray a la eeth-kyair-da

Turn right
gire a la derecha
hee-ray a la de-ray-cha

You have to go back
Tiene que dar la vuelta
tee-e-nay kay dar la bwel-ta

Directions

Take the first road on the right
Coja la primera carretera a la derecha
ko-ha la pree-mair-a ka-re-tair-a a la de-ray-cha

Take the road for Simancas
Coja la carretera de Simancas
ko-ha la ka-re-tair-a day see-man-kas

Take the second road on the left
Coja la segunda carretera a la izquierda
ko-ha la se-goon-da ka-re-tair-a a la eeth-kyair-da

Hiring a car

I want to hire a car
Quiero alquilar un coche
kee-e-ro al-kee-lar oon ko-chay

I need it for 2 weeks
Lo quiero para dos semanas
lo kee-e-ro pa-ra dos se-ma-nas

Can I hire a car?
¿Es posible alquilar un coche?
es po-see-blay al-kee-lar oon ko-chay

Can I hire a car with an automatic gearbox?
¿Puedo alquilar un coche con cambio automático?
pwe-do al-kee-lar oon ko-chay kon kam-byo ow-to-ma-tee-ko

Please explain the documents
Por favor, explíqueme los documentos
por fa-bor, eks-plee-kay-may los do-koo-men-tos

Hiring a car

We will both be driving
Conduciremos los dos
kon-doo-thee-ray-mos los dos

Do you have — a large car?
       ¿Tiene — un coche grande?
    tee-e-nay — oon ko-chay gran-day

              — a smaller car?
              — un coche más pequeño?
              — *oon ko-chay mas pe-ken-yo*

              — an automatic?
              — un coche con cambio automático?
              — *oon ko-chay kon kam-byo ow-to-ma-tee-ko*

              — an estate car?
              — una furgoneta?
              — *oo-na foor-go-nay-ta*

I want to leave a car at the airport
Quiero dejar el coche en el aeropuerto
kee-e-ro de-har el ko-chay en el a-air-o-pwair-to

I would like to leave the car at the airport
Me gustaría dejar el coche en el aeropuerto
may goo-sta-ree-a de-har el ko-chay en el a-air-o-pwair-to

Is there a charge per kilometre?
¿Se cobra el kilometraje?
say ko-bra el kee-lo-me-tra-hay

Must I return the car here?
¿Tengo que devolver el coche aquí?
ten-go kay de-bol-bair el ko-chay a-kee

Hiring a car

Can I pay for insurance?
¿Puedo pagar un seguro?
pwe-do pa-gar oon se-goo-ro

Do I have to pay a deposit?
¿Tengo que pagar algún depósito?
ten-go kay pa-gar oon de-po-zee-to

How does the steering lock work?
¿Cómo funciona el antirrobo?
ko-mo foon-thyo-na el an-tee-ro-bo

I would like a spare set of keys
Me gustaría tener un juego de llaves de repuesto
may goo-sta-ree-a te-nair oon hway-go day ya-bes day re-pwes-to

Where is reverse gear?
¿Dónde está la marcha atrás?
don-day es-ta la mar-cha a-tras

Where is the tool kit?
¿Dónde está la caja de herramientas?
don-day es-ta la ka-ha day e-ra-myen-tas

Please show me how to — operate the lights
Por favor, enséñeme cómo — manejar las luces
por fa-bor, en-sen-yay-may ko-mo — ma-ne-har las loo-thes

— operate the windscreen wipers
— manejar los limpiaparabrisas
— ma-ne-har los leem-pya-pa-ra-bree-sas

By taxi

Where can I get a taxi?
¿Dónde puedo tomar un taxi?
don-day pwe-do to-mar oon tak-see

Take me to the airport, please
Lléveme al aeropuerto, por favor
ye-bay-may al a-air-o-pwair-to, por fa-bor

The bus station, please
La estación de autobuses, por favor
la es-ta-thyon day ow-to-boo-ses, por fa-bor

Please show us around the town
Por favor, enséñenos la ciudad
por fa-bor, en-sen-yay-nos la thee-oo-dad

Please take me to this address
Por favor, lléveme a esta dirección
por fa-bor, ye-bay-may a es-ta dee-rek-thyon

Could you put the bags in the boot, please?
Puede meter las bolsas en el maletero, por favor
pwe-day me-tair las bol-sas en el ma-le-te-ro, por fa-bor

Turn left, please
Gire a la izquierda, por favor
hee-ray a la eeth-kyair-da, por fa-bor

Turn right, please
Gire a la derecha, por favor
hee-ray a la de-ray-cha, por fa-bor

By taxi

Wait for me please
Espéreme, por favor
es-pe-ray-may, por fa-bor

Can you come back in one hour?
¿Puede volver dentro de una hora?
pwe-day bol-bair den-tro day oo-na o-ra

Please wait here for a few minutes
Por favor, espere aquí unos minutos
por fa-bor, es-pe-ray a-kee oo-nos mee-noo-tos

Please, stop at the corner
Por favor, pare en la esquina
por fa-bor, pa-ray en la es-kee-na

Please, wait here
Espere aquí, por favor
es-pe-ray a-kee, por fa-bor

I am in a hurry
Tengo prisa
ten-go pree-sa

Please hurry, I am late
Dése prisa por favor, se me ha hecho tarde
day-say pree-sa por fa-bor, say may a e-cho tar-day

How much is it per kilometre?
¿Cuánto cuesta por kilómetro?
kwan-to kwes-ta por kee-lo-me-tro

How much is that, please?
¿Cuánto es eso, por favor?
kwan-to es e-so, por fa-bor

Keep the change
Quédese con el cambio
kay-day-say kon el kam-byo

By bus

Does this bus go to the castle?
¿Este autobús va al castillo?
es-tay ow-to-boos ba al ka-stee-yo

How frequent is the service?
¿Con qué frecuencia es el servicio?
kon kay fre-kwen-thee-a es el sair-bee-thee-o

What is the fare to the city centre?
¿Cuánto es al centro de la ciudad?
kwan-to es al then-tro day la thee-oo-dad

Where should I change?
¿Dónde tengo que cambiar?
don-day ten-go kay kam-byar

Which bus do I take for the football stadium?
¿Qué autobús tengo que coger para el estadio de fútbol?
*kay ow-to-boos ten-go kay ko-hair pa-ra el es-ta-dee-o day
foot-bol*

Where do I get the bus for the airport?
¿Dónde puedo coger el autobús para el aeropuerto?
*don-day pwe-do ko-hair el ow-to-boos pa-ra el a-air-o-
pwair-to*

By bus

Will you tell me when to get off the bus?
¿Me dirá cuándo bajarme del autobús?
may dee-ra kwan-do ba-har-may del ow-to-boos

When is the last bus?
¿Á que hora es el último autobús?
a kay o-ra es el ool-tee-mo ow-to-boos

By train

Can I buy a return ticket?
¿Puedo comprar un billete de ida y vuelta?
pwe-do kom-prar oon bee-ye-tay day ee-da ee bwel-ta

A return (round-trip ticket) to Barcelona, please
Un billete de ida y vuelta a Barcelona, por favor
oon bee-ye-tay day ee-da ee bwel-ta a bar-the-lo-na, por fa-bor

A return to Paris, first class
Un billete de ida y vuelta a París, en primera clase
oon bee-ye-tay day ee-da ee bwel-ta a pa-rees, en pree-mair-a kla-say

A single (one-way ticket) to Lisbon, please
Un billete de ida a Lisboa, por favor
oon bee-ye-tay day ee-da a leez-bo-a, por fa-bor

A smoking compartment, first-class
Compartimento de fumadores, primera clase
kom-par-tee-men-to day foo-ma-do-res, pree-mair-a kla-say

By train

A non-smoking compartment, please
Compartimento de no fumadores, por favor
kom-par-tee-men-to day no foo-ma-do-res, por fa-bor

Second class. A window seat, please
En segunda. Asiento de ventana, por favor
en se-goon-da. a-syen-to day ben-ta-na, por fa-bor

Can I take my bicycle?
¿Puedo llevar mi bicicleta?
pwe-do ye-bar mee bee-thee-klay-ta

Is this the platform for Zaragoza?
¿Es ésta el andén para Zaragoza?
es es-ta el an-den pa-ra tha-ra-go-tha

What are the times of the trains to Paris?
¿Cuál es el horario de trenes para París?
kwal es el o-ra-ree-o day tre-nes pa-ra pa-rees

How long do I have before my next train leaves?
¿Cuánto tiempo tengo antes de mi próximo tren?
kwan-to tee-em-po ten-go an-tes day mee prok-see-mo tren

Where can I buy a ticket?
¿Dónde puedo comprar un billete?
don-day pwe-do kom-prar oon bee-ye-tay

Where do I have to change?
¿Dónde tengo que cambiar?
don-day ten-go kay kam-byar

Where do I pick up my bags?
¿Dónde se recogen los equipajes?
don-day say re-ko-hen los e-kee-pa-hays

By train

Can I check in my bags?
¿Puedo facturar el equipaje?
pwe-do fak-too-rar el e-kee-pa-hay

I want to leave these bags in the left-luggage
Quiero dejar estas bolsas en la consigna
kee-e-ro de-har es-tas bol-sas en la kon-seeg-na

How much is it per bag?
¿Cuánto es por cada bolsa?
kwan-to es por ka-da bol-sa

I shall pick them up this evening
Las recogeré esta tarde
las re-ko-hair-ay es-ta tar-day

I want to book a seat on the Sleeper to Paris
Quiero reservar una plaza en coche-cama a París
kee-e-o re-sair-bar oo-na pla-tha en ko-chay-ka-ma a pa-rees

Is there — a left-luggage office?
  ¿Hay — consigna de equipajes?
  a-ee — kon-seeg-na day e-kee-pa-hes

    — a buffet car (club car)?
    — coche bar?
    — ko-chay bar

    — a dining car?
    — vagón restaurante?
    — ba-gon re-sto-ran-tay

    — a restaurant on the train?
    — coche restaurante en el tren?
    — ko-chay re-sto-ran-tay en el tren

By train

Where is the departure board (listing)?
¿Dónde está el tablón de salidas?
don-day es-ta el ta-blon day sa-lee-das

What time does the train leave?
¿A qué hora sale el tren?
a kay o-ra sa-lay el tren

Do I have time to go shopping?
¿Tengo tiempo para ir de compras?
ten-go tee-em-po pa-ra eer day kom-pras

What time is the last train?
¿A qué hora es el último tren?
a kay o-ra es el ool-tee-mo el tren

When is the next train to Seville?
¿Cuándo sale el siguiente tren para Sevilla?
kwan-do sa-lay el see-gee-en-tay tren pa-ra se-bee-ya

When is the next train to Valencia?
¿Cuándo es el siguiente tren para Valencia?
kwan-do sa-lay el see-gee-en-tay tren pa-ra ba-len-thee-a

Which platform do I go to?
¿A qué andén tengo que ir?
a kay an-den ten-go kay eer

Is this a through train?
¿Es éste un tren directo?
es es-tay oon tren dee-rek-to

Is this the Madrid train?
¿Es éste el tren de Madrid?
es es-tay el tren day ma-dreed

By train

Do we stop at Vigo?
¿Paramos en Vigo?
pa-ra-mos en bee-go

What time do we get to Burgos?
¿A qué hora llegamos a Burgos?
a kay o-ra ye-ga-mos a boor-gos

Are we at Durango yet?
¿Hemos llegado a Durango?
ay-mos ye-ga-do a doo-ran-go

Are we on time?
¿Llegaremos a la hora prevista?
ye-ga-ray-mos a la o-ra pray-bee-sta

Can you help me with my bags?
Puede ayudarme con el equipaje?
pwe-day a-yoo-dar-may kon el e-kee-pa-hay

Is this seat taken?
¿Está ocupado este asiento?
es-ta o-koo-pa-do es-tay a-syen-to

May I open the window?
¿Le importa si abro la ventana?
lay eem-por-ta see a-bro la ben-ta-na

My wife has my ticket
Mi esposa tiene mi billete
mee es-po-sa tee-e-nay mee bee-ye-tay

I have lost my ticket
He perdido el billete
ay pair-dee-do el bee-ye-tay

This is a non-smoking compartment
Éste es un compartimento de no fumadores
es-tay es oon kom-par-tee-men-to day no foo-ma-do-res

This is my seat
Éste es mi asiento
es-tay es mee a-syen-to

Where is the toilet?
¿Dónde está el servicio?
don-day es-ta el sair-bee-thee-o

Why have we stopped?
¿Por qué hemos parado?
por kay ay-mos pa-ra-do

DRIVING

Traffic and weather conditions

Are there any hold-ups?
¿Hay atascos?
a-ee a-tas-kos

Is the traffic heavy?
¿Hay mucho tráfico?
a-ee moo-cho tra-fee-ko

Is the traffic one-way?
¿Es sentido único?
es sen-tee-do oo-nee-ko

Is there a different way to the stadium?
¿Hay otro camino al estadio?
a-ee o-tro ka-mee-no al es-ta-dee-o

Is there a toll on this motorway (highway)?
¿Esta autopista es de peaje?
es-ta ow-to-pee-sta es day pay-a-hay

What is causing this traffic jam?
¿Qué está causando éste embotellamiento?
kay es-ta kow-san-do es-tay em-bo-te-ya-myen-to

What is the speed limit?
¿Cuál es el límite de velocidad?
kwal es el lee-mee-tay day be-lo-thee-dad

What time does the car park close?
¿Cuándo se cierra el parking?
kwan-do say thee-e-ra el par-keen

When is the rush hour?
¿Cuándo es la hora punta?
kwan-do es la o-ra poon-ta

Do I need snow chains?
¿Necesito cadenas para la nieve?
ne-the-see-to ka-day-nas pa-ra la nee-e-bay

Is the pass open?
¿Está el paso abierto?
es-ta el pa-so a-bee-air-to

Is the road to Segovia snowed up?
¿Está nevada la carretera a Segovia?
es-ta ne-ba-da la ka-re-tair-a a se-go-bee-a

When will the road be clear?
¿Cuándo estará la carretera despejada?
kwan-do es-ta-ra la ka-re-tair-a des-pe-ha-da

Parking

Is it safe to park here?
¿Es seguro aparcar aquí?
es se-goo-ro a-par-kar a-kee

Can I park here?
¿Puedo aparcar aquí?
pwe-do a-par-kar a-kee

Do I need a parking disc?
¿Necesito ficha de aparcamiento?
ne-the-see-to fee-cha day a-par-ka-myen-to

Parking

Where can I get a parking disc?
¿Dónde puedo obtener una ficha de aparcamiento?
don-day pwe-do ob-te-nair oo-na fee-cha day a-par-ka-myen-to

Where do I pay?
¿Dónde tengo que pagar?
don-day ten-go kay pa-gar

Where is there a car park (parking lot)?
¿Dónde hay un aparcamiento?
don-day a-ee oon a-par-ka-myen-to

How long can I stay here?
¿Cuánto tiempo puedo permanecer aquí?
kwan-to tee-em-po pwe-do pair-ma-ne-thair a-kee

Do I need — coins for the meter?
¿Necesito — monedas para el parquímetro?
ne-the-see-to — mo-nay-das pa-ra el par-kee-me-tro

— parking lights?
— luces de posición?
— loo-thes day po-zee-thyon

At the service station

Do you take credit cards?
¿Acepta tarjetas de crédito?
a-thep-ta tar-hay-tas day kre-dee-to

Can you clean the windscreen?
¿Puede limpiar el parabrisas?
pwe-day leem-pyar el pa-ra-bree-sas

At the service station

Fill the tank please
Llene el depósito, por favor
ye-nay el de-po-zee-to, por fa-bor

25 litres of — unleaded petrol
Veinticinco litros de — gasolina sin plomo
bain-tee-theen-ko lee-tros day — ga-so-lee-na seen plo-mo

— 3 star
— normal
— nor-mal

— 4 star
— super
— soo-pair

— diesel
— gas-oil
— ga-zoil

I need some distilled water
Necesito agua destilada
ne-the-see-to a-gwa de-stee-la-da

Check the tyre pressure please
Revise la presión de los neumáticos, por favor
re-bee-say la pre-syon day los nay-oo-ma-tee-kos, por fa-bor

The pressure should be 2.3 at the front and 2.5 at the rear
La presión debería estar en dos coma tres en los
delanteros y dos coma cinco en los traseros
*la pre-syon de-be-ree-a es-tar en dos ko-ma tres en los
de-lan-tair-os ee dos ko-ma theen-ko en los tra-sair-os*

At the service station

Check — the oil
Revise — el aceite
re-bee-say — el a-thay-ee-tay

— **the water**
— el agua
— *el a-gwa*

Breakdowns and repairs

Can you give me — a push?
¿Puede — empujarme?
pwe-day — em-poo-har-may

— **a tow?**
— remolcarme?
— *re-mol-kar-may*

Can you send a recovery truck?
¿Puede enviar un camión grúa?
pwe-day en-byar oon ka-myon groo-a

Can you take me to the nearest garage?
¿Puede llevarme al garage más cercano?
pwe-day ye-bar-may al ga-ra-hay mas thair-ka-no

Is there a telephone nearby?
¿Hay algún teléfono cercano?
a-ee al-goon te-le-fo-no thair-ka-no

Can you find out what the trouble is?
¿Puede encontrar el problema?
pwe-day en-kon-trar el pro-blay-ma

Breakdowns and repairs

Can you give me a can of petrol, please?
¿Me da un bidón de gasolina, por favor?
*may da oon bee-**don** day ga-so-**lee**-na, por fa-**bor***

Can you repair a flat tyre?
¿Puede reparar una rueda desinflada?
*pwe-day re-pa-**rar** oo-na roo-**ay**-da des-een-**fla**-da*

Can you repair it for the time being?
¿Puede repararlo provisionalmente?
*pwe-day re-pa-**rar**-lo pro-bees-yo-nal-**men**-tay*

Can you replace the windscreen wiper blades?
¿Puede cambiar las paletas del limpiaparabrisas?
*pwe-day kam-**byar** las pa-**lay**-tas del leem-pya-pa-ra-**bree**-sas*

My car has broken down
Mi coche se ha averiado
*mee ko-chay say a a-be-ree-**a**-do*

My car will not start
Mi coche no arranca
*mee ko-chay no a-**ran**-ka*

Do you have an emergency fan belt?
Tiene una correa de ventilador de emergencia?
*tee-e-nay oo-na ko-**ray**-a day ben-tee-la-**dor** day e-mair-**hen**-thee-a*

Do you have jump leads?
¿Tiene cables puente de batería?
*tee-e-nay **ka**-bles **pwen**-tay day ba-te-**ree**-a*

Do you have the spare parts?
¿Tiene los repuestos?
*tee-e-nay los re-**pwe**-stos*

Breakdowns and repairs

I have a flat tyre
Tengo un pinchazo
ten-go oon peen-cha-tho

I have blown a fuse
Se me ha quemado un fusible
say may a ke-ma-do oon foo-see-blay

I have locked myself out of the car
He cerrado el coche con las llaves dentro
ay the-ra-do el ko-chay kon las ya-bes den-tro

I have locked the ignition key inside the car
He dejado la llave de contacto dentro del coche
ay de-ha-do la ya-bay day kon-tak-to den-tro del ko-chay

I have run out of petrol
Me he quedado sin gasolina
may ay ke-da-do seen ga-so-lee-na

I need a new fan belt
Necesito una nueva correa de ventilador
ne-the-see-to oo-na nway-ba ko-ray-a day ben-tee-la-dor

I think there is a bad connection
Creo que hay una mala conexión
kray-o kay a-ee oo-na ma-la ko-nek-syon

Is there a mechanic here?
¿Hay algún mecánico aquí?
a-ee al-goon me-ka-nee-ko a-kee

The engine has broken down
Se ha averiado el motor
say a a-be-ree-a-do el mo-tor

Breakdowns and repairs

There is something wrong
Hay algún problema
a-ee al-goon pro-blay-ma

There is something wrong with the car
Algo va mal en el coche
al-go ba mal en el ko-chay

Will it take long to repair it?
¿Tardará mucho en repararlo?
tar-da-ra moo-cho en re-pa-rar-lo

Is it serious?
¿Es grave?
es gra-bay

My windscreen has cracked
Se me ha rajado el parabrisas
say may a ra-ha-do el pa-ra-bree-sas

The air-conditioning does not work
No funciona el aire acondicionado
no foon-thyo-na el a-ee-ray a-kon-dee-thyo-na-do

The battery is flat
La batería está descargada
la ba-te-ree-a es-ta des-kar-ga-da

The engine is overheating
El motor se recalienta
el mo-tor say re-ka-lyen-ta

The exhaust pipe has fallen off
Se ha caído el tubo de escape
say a ky-ee-do el too-bo day es-ka-pay

Breakdowns and repairs

There is a leak in the radiator
Hay una fuga en el radiador
a-ee oo-na foo-ga en el ra-dee-a-dor

Accidents and the Police

There has been an accident
Ha habido un accidente
*a a-**bee**-do oon ak-thee-**den**-tay*

We must call an ambulance
Tenemos que llamar a una ambulancia
*te-**nay**-mos kay ya-**mar** a **oo**-na am-boo-**lan**-thee-a*

We must call the police
Tenemos que llamar a la policía
*te-**nay**-mos kay ya-**mar** a la po-lee-**thee**-a*

What is your name and address?
¿Cuál es su nombre y direción?
*kwal es soo **nom**-bray ee dee-rek-**thyon***

You must not move
No debe moverse
*no **de**-bay mo-**bair**-say*

Do you want my passport?
¿Quiere mi pasaporte?
*kee-e-ray mee pa-sa-**por**-tay*

He did not stop
Él no paró
*el no pa-**ro***

Accidents and the Police

He is a witness
Éste es testigo
es-tay es te-stee-go

He overtook on a bend
Él adelantó en una curva
el a-de-lan-to en la coor-ba

He ran into the back of my car
Él chocó con la parte trasera de mi coche
el cho-ko kon la par-tay tra-sair-a day mee ko-chay

He stopped suddenly
Él se paró de repente
el say pa-ro day re-pen-tay

He was moving too fast
Él iba demasiado rápido
el ee-ba de-ma-sya-a-do ra-pee-do

Here are my insurance documents
Aquí está la documentación del seguro
a-kee es-ta la do-koo-men-ta-thyon del se-goo-ro

Here is my driving licence
Aquí está mi permiso de conducir
a-kee es-ta mee pair-mee-so day kon-doo-theer

I could not stop in time
No he podido parar a tiempo
no ay po-dee-do pa-rar a tee-em-po

I did not see the bicycle
No vi la bicicleta
no bee la bee-thee-klay-ta

Accidents and the Police

I did not see the sign
No vi la señal
no bee la sen-yal

I did not understand the sign
No entendí la señal
no en-ten-dee la sen-yal

I am very sorry. I am a visitor
Lo siento mucho. Soy turista
lo syen-to moo-cho. Soy too-ree-sta

I did not know about the speed limit
No sabía lo del límite de velocidad
no sa-bee-a lo del lee-mee-tay day be-lo-thee-dad

How much is the fine?
¿Cuánto es la multa?
kwan-to es la mool-ta

I have not got enough money. Can I pay at the police station?
No tengo suficiente dinero ¿Puedo pagar en la comisaría de policía?
no ten-go soo-fee-thee-en-tay dee-ne-ro. Pwe-do pa-gar en la ko-mee-sa-ree-a day po-lee-thee-a

I have not had anything to drink
No he bebido nada
no ay be-bee-do na-da

I was only driving at 50 km/h
Sólo iba a cincuenta por hora
so-lo ee-ba a theen-kwen-ta por o-ra

Accidents and the Police

I was overtaking
Estaba adelantando
es-ta-ba a-de-lan-tan-do

I was parking
Estaba aparcando
es-ta-ba a-par-kan-do

My car has been towed away
La grúa se ha llevado mi coche
la groo-a say a ye-ba-do mee ko-chay

That car was too close
Ese coche venía demasiado cerca
e-say ko-chay be-nee-a de-ma-sya-do thair-ka

The brakes failed
Los frenos fallaron
los fray-nos fa-ya-ron

The car number (license number) was...
La matrícula del coche era...
la ma-tree-koo-la del ko-chay ay-ra...

The car skidded
El coche derrapó
el ko-chay de-ra-po

The car swerved
El coche giró bruscamente
el ko-chay hee-ro broo-ska-men-tay

The car turned right without signalling
El coche giró a la derecha sin señalizar
el ko-chay hee-ro a la de-ray-cha seen sen-ya-lee-thar

Accidents and the Police

The road was icy
La carretera estaba conjelada
*la ka-re-**tair**-a es-**ta**-ba kon-he-**la**-da*

The tyre burst
El neumático reventó
*el nay-oo-**ma**-tee-ko re-ben-**to***

Car parts

accelerator
acelerador
*a-the-le-ra-**dor***

aerial
antena
*an-**tay**-na*

air filter
filtro de aire
***feel**-tro day a-ee-ray*

alternator
alternador
*al-tair-na-**dor***

antifreeze
anti-congelante
*an-tee-kon-he-**lan**-tay*

axle
eje
e-hay

battery
batería
*ba-te-**ree**-a*

bonnet
capó
*ka-**po***

boot
maletero
*ma-le-**te**-ro*

brake fluid
líquido de frenos
***lee**-kee-do day **fray**-nos*

brakes
frenos
***fray**-nos*

bulb
foco
***fo**-ko*

Car parts

bumper
parachoques
pa-ra-cho-kes

car-phone
teléfono de automóvil
te-le-fo-no day ow-to-mo-beel

carburettor
carburador
kar-boo-ra-dor

child seat
silla de niño
see-ya day neen-yo

choke
estárter
e-star-tair

clutch
embrague
em-bra-gay

cylinder
cilindro
thee-leen-dro

disc brake
freno de disco
fray-no day dee-sko

distributor
distribuidor
dees-tree-boo-ee-dor

door
portazuela
por-ta-thway-la

dynamo
dinamo
dee-na-mo

electrical system
sistema eléctrico
see-stay-ma e-lek-tree-ko

engine
motor
mo-tor

exhaust system
sistema de escape
see-stay-ma day e-ska-pay

fan belt
correa del ventilador
ko-ray-a del ben-tee-la-dor

foot pump
bomba de pie
bom-ba day pee-ay

fuse
fusible
foo-see-blay

fuel pump
bomba de carburante
bom-ba day kar-boo-ran-tay

Car parts

fuel gauge
indicador de carburante
*een-dee-ka-**dor** day kar-boo-**ran**-tay*

gear box
caja de cambios
***ka**-ha day **kam**-bee-os*

gear lever
palanca de cambios
*pa-**lan**-ka day **kam**-bee-os*

generator
generador
*he-ne-ra-**dor***

hammer
martillo
*mar-**tee**-yo*

hand brake
freno de mano
***fray**-no day **ma**-no*

headlights
faros
***fa**-ros*

hood
capó
*ka-**po***

hazard lights
luces de emergencia
***loo**-thes day e-mair-**hen**-thee-a*

horn
bocina
*bo-**thee**-na*

hose
manga
***man**-ga*

ignition
contacto
*kon-**tak**-to*

ignition key
llave de contacto
*ya-bay day kon-**tak**-to*

indicator
intermitente
*een-tair-mee-**ten**-tay*

jack
gato
***ga**-to*

lights
luces
***loo**-thes*

Car parts

lock
cerradura
the-ra-doo-ra

muffler
silenciador
see-len-thee-a-dor

oil
aceite
a-thay-ee-tay

oil filter
filtro de aceite
feel-tro day a-thay-ee-tay

oil pressure
presión de aceite
pre-syon day a-thay-ee-tay

petrol
gasolina
ga-so-lee-na

points
platinos
pla-tee-nos

pump
bomba
bom-ba

radiator
radiador
ra-dee-a-dor

rear view mirror
espejo retrovisor
es-pe-ho re-tro-bee-sor

reflectors
reflectantes
re-flek-tan-tes

reversing light
luz de marcha atrás
looth day mar-cha a-tras

roof-rack
baca
ba-ka

screwdriver
destornillador
des-tor-nee-ya-dor

seat
asiento
a-syen-to

seat belt
cinturón de seguridad
then-too-ron day se-goo-ree-dad

shock absorber
amortiguador
a-mor-tee-gwa-dor

silencer
silenciador
see-len-thee-a-dor

Car parts

socket set
juego de llaves de tubo
hway-go day ya-bes day too-bo

spanner
llave inglesa
ya-bay een-glay-sa

spare part
repuesto
re-pwe-sto

spark plug
bujía
boo-hee-a

speedometer
velocímetro
be-lo-thee-me-tro

starter motor
motor de arranque
mo-tor day a-ran-kay

steering
dirección
dee-rek-thyon

steering wheel
volante
bo-lan-tay

stoplight
luz de freno
looth day fray-no

sun roof
techo solar
te-cho so-lar

suspension
suspensión
soo-spen-syon

tools
herramientas
e-ra-myen-tas

towbar
barra de remolque
ba-ra day re-mol-kay

transmission
transmisión
trans-mee-syon

trunk
maletero
ma-le-te-ro

tyre
neumático
nay-oo-ma-tee-ko

warning light
luz de advertencia
looth day ad-bair-ten-thee-a

wheel
rueda
roo-ay-da

windscreen
parabrisas
*pa-ra-**bree**-sas*

wipers
limpiaparabrisas
*leem-pya-pa-ra-**bree**-sas*

windshield
parabrisas
*pa-ra-**bree**-sas*

wrench
llave inglesa
*ya-bay een-**glay**-sa*

Road signs

aparcamiento sólo para residentes
parking for residents only
*a-par-ka-**myen**-to **so**-lo pa-ra re-see-**den**-tes*

desviación
diversion
*des-bee-a-**thyon***

circule por la derecha
keep to the right
*theer-**koo**-lay por la de-**ray**-cha*

camino particular
private road
*ka-**mee**-no par-tee-koo-**lar***

prohibido el paso
no thoroughfare
*pro-ee-**bee**-do el **pa**-so*

no entrar
no entry
*no en-**trar***

EATING OUT

Reservations

Should we reserve a table?
¿Deberíamos reservar mesa?
*de-be-**ree**-a-mos re-sair-**bar** **may**-sa*

Can I book a table for four at 8 o'clock?
¿Podría reservar una mesa para cuatro para las ocho?
*po-**dree**-a re-sair-**bar** oo-na **may**-sa pa-ra **kwa**-tro pa-ra las **o**-cho*

Can we have a table for four?
Una mesa para cuatro, por favor
*oo-na **may**-sa pa-ra **kwa**-tro, por fa-**bor***

I am a vegetarian
Soy vegetariano (vegeterania)
*soy be-he-ta-**ree**-a-no (be-he-ta-**ree**-a-na)*

We would like a table — by the window
Nos gustaría una mesa — junto a la ventana
*nos goo-sta-**ree**-a oo-na **may**-sa — **hoon**-to a la ben-**ta**-na*

— on the terrace
— en la terraza
*— en la te-**ra**-tha*

Useful questions

Are vegetables included?
¿Se incluye verdura?
*say een-**kloo**-yay bair-**doo**-ra*

Useful questions

Do you have a local speciality?
¿Tienen alguna especialidad local?
tee-e-nen al-goo-na es-peth-ya-lee-dad lo-kal

Do you have a set menu?
¿Tiene un menú del día?
tee-e-nay oon me-noo del dee-a

What do you recommend?
¿Qué me recomienda?
kay may re-ko-myen-da

What is the dish of the day?
¿Cuál es el plato del día?
kwal es el pla-to del dee-a

What is the soup of the day?
¿Cuál es la sopa del día?
kwal es la so-pa del dee-a

What is this called?
¿Cómo se llama esto?
ko-mo say ya-ma es-to

What is this dish like?
¿Cómo es este plato?
ko-mo es es-tay pla-to

Which local wine do you recommend?
¿Qué vino local recomienda?
kay bee-no lo-kal re-ko-myen-da

Do you have yoghurt?
¿Tiene yogur?
tee-e-nay yo-goor

Useful questions

How do I eat this?
¿Cómo se come esto?
ko-mo say ko-may es-to

Is the local wine good?
¿Es bueno el vino local?
es bway-no el bee-no lo-kal

Is this cheese very strong?
¿Es muy fuerte este queso?
es mwee fwair-tay es-tay ke-so

Is this good?
¿Está bueno esto?
es-ta bway-no es-to

What is this?
¿Qué es esto?
kay es es-to

Ordering your meal

The menu, please
El menú, por favor
el me-noo, por fa-bor

I will take the set menu
Tomaré el menú del día
to-ma-ray el me-noo del dee-a

Can we start with soup?
¿Podemos empezar con sopa?
po-day-mos em-pe-thar kon so-pa

Ordering your meal

I like my steak — very rare
    Me gusta — muy poco hecho
    *may **goo**-sta — mwee **po**-ko e-cho*

                — rare
                — poco hecho
                *— **po**-ko e-cho*

                — medium rare
                — medianamente hecho
                *— me-dee-a-na-**men**-tay e-cho*

                — well done
                — bien hecho
                — bee-en e-cho

Could we have some butter?
¿Puede traernos mantequilla , por favor?
*pwe-day try-**air**-nos man-te-**kee**-ya, por fa-**bor***

We need some bread, please
Nos hace falta pan, por favor
*nos **a**-thay **fal**-ta pan, por fa-**bor***

I will have salad
Yo tomaré ensalada
*yo to-ma-**ray** en-sa-**la**-da*

I will take that
Tomaré eso
*to-ma-**ray** e-so*

That is for me
Eso es para mí
*e-so es **pa**-ra mee*

Ordering your meal

Could we have some more bread please?
¿Puede traernos más pan por favor?
pwe-day try-air-nos mas pan, por fa-bor

Can I see the menu again, please?
¿Puedo volver a ver el menú, por favor?
pwe-do bol-bair a bair el me-noo, por fa-bor

Ordering drinks

The wine list, please
La lista de vinos, por favor
la lee-sta day bee-nos, por fa-bor

We will take the Rioja
Tomaremos el Rioja
to-ma-ray-mos el ree-o-ha

A bottle of house red wine, please
Una botella de vino tinto de la casa
oo-na bo-te-ya day bee-no teen-to day la ka-sa

A glass of dry white wine, please
Un vaso de vino blanco seco, por favor
oon ba-so day bee-no blan-ko se-ko, por fa-bor

Another bottle of red wine, please
Otra botella de vino tinto, por favor
o-tra bo-te-ya day bee-no teen-to, por fa-bor

Another glass, please
Otro vaso, por favor
o-tro ba-so, por fa-bor

Black coffee, please
Café sólo, por favor
ka-fay so-lo, por fa-bor

Can we have some mineral water?
¿Nos puede traer agua mineral?
nos pwe-day try-air a-gwa mee-ne-ral

Coffee with milk, please
Café con leche, por favor
ka-fay kon le-chay, por fa-bor

Some plain water, please
Agua natural, por favor
a-gwa na-too-ral, por fa-bor

Two beers, please
Dos cervezas, por favor
dos thair-bay-thas, por fa-bor

Paying the bill

Can we have the bill, please?
¿Puede traernos la cuenta, por favor?
pwe-day try-air-nos la kwen-ta, por fa-bor

Is service included?
¿Está el servicio incluido?
es-ta el sair-bee-thee-o een-kloo-ee-do

Is tax included?
¿Están los impuestos incluidos?
es-tan los eem-pwe-stos een-kloo-ee-dos

Paying the bill

Is there any extra charge?
¿Hay algún cargo adicional?
a-ee al-goon kar-go a-deeth-yo-nal

I haven't enough money
No tengo suficiente dinero
no ten-go soo-feeth-yen-tay dee-ne-ro

This is not correct
Esto no es correcto
es-to no es ko-rek-to

This is not my bill
Esta no es mi cuenta
es-ta no es mee kwen-ta

You have given me the wrong change
Me ha dado mal los cambios
may a da-do mal los kam-bee-os

Complaints and compliments

This is cold
Esto está frio
es-to es-ta free-o

This is not what I ordered
Esto no es lo que he pedido
es-to no es lo kay ay pe-dee-do

Waiter! We have been waiting for a long time
¡Camarero! Estamos esperando desde hace mucho
ka-ma-rair-o! Es-ta-mos es-pe-ran-do dez-day a-thay moo-cho tee-em-po

Menu reader

Can I have the recipe?
¿Puede darme la receta?
pwe-day dar-may la re-thay-ta

The meal was excellent
La comida estaba excelente
la ko-mee-da es-ta-ba eks-the-len-tay

This is excellent
Esto está buenísimo
es-to es-ta bwe-nee-see-mo

Menu reader

aceite
a-thay-ee-tay
oil

albahaca
al-ba-a-ka
basil

aceitunas
a-thay-too-nas
olives

albaricoques
al-ba-ree-ko-kes
apricots

acelga
a-thel-ga
chard

albondigas
al-bon-dee-gas
meatballs

aguacate
a-gwa-ka-tay
avocado

alcachofa
al-ka-cho-fa
artichoke

ajo
a-ho
garlic

almejas
al-may-has
clams

Menu reader

antequilla
mman-te-kee-ya
butter

apio
a-pee-o
celery

arroz con leche
a-roth kon le-chay
rice pudding

asada/a la parrilla
a-sa-da/a la pa-ree-ya
grilled/barbecued

atún
a-toon
tuna

berenjena
be-ren-hay-na
aubergine

berenjena
be-ren-hay-na
eggplant

berro
be-ro
watercress

berza
ber-tha
cabbage

bizcocho
beeth-ko-cho
sponge cake

bogavante a la marinera
bo-ga-ban-tay a la ma-ree-nair-a
lobster cooked in Galician style

budín
boo-deen
pudding

buñuelos
boon-yoo-ay-los
doughnuts

caballa
ka-ba-ya
mackerel

caballa en escabeche
ka-ba-ya en es-ka-be-chay
marinated mackerel

cabezas de cordero al horno
ka-bay-thas day kor-dair-o al or-no
roast head of lamb (Aragon)

calabacín
ka-la-ba-theen
courgette

Menu reader

calabaza
ka-la-ba-tha
squash

calamares
ka-la-ma-res
squid

caldo
kal-do
broth

caldo de pollo
kal-do day po-yo
chicken broth

caldo de vaca
kal-do day ba-ka
beef broth

callos
ka-yos
tripe

cangrejo de rio
kan-gre-ho day ree-o
crayfish

carne
kar-nay
meat

carne asada
kar-nay a-sa-da
grilled meats

carne de vaca en asador
kar-nay day ba-ka en a-sa-dor
braised beef

castañas asadas
kas-tan-yas a-sa-das
roast chestnuts

cebollas
the-bo-yas
onions

cebollinos
the-bo-yee-nos
chives

cerdo asado
thair-do a-sa-do
pork roast

cerezas
thair-ay-thas
cherries

chalotes
cha-lo-tes
shallots

champiñones
cham-peen-yo-nes
mushrooms

champiñones al ajillo
cham-peen-yo-nes al a-hee-yo
mushrooms with garlic

Menu reader

champiñones en salsa
cham-peen-yo-nes en sal-sa
mushrooms in sauce

chirivía
chee-ree-bee-a
parsnip

chuleta corriente
choo-lay-ta ko-ree-en-tay
plain cutlet

chuleta de cerdo
choo-lay-ta day thair-do
pork cutlet

chuleta de cordero
choo-lay-ta day kor-dair-o
lamb cutlet

chuleta de ternera
choo-lay-ta day tair-nair-a
veal cutlet

churros
choo-ros
fritters

ciruelas
thee-roo-ay-las
plums

ciruelas claudias
thee-roo-e-ay-las clow-dee-as
greengages

cochinillo asado
ko-chee-nee-yo a-sa-do
roast suckling pig (Castile)

cocido de alubias
ko-thee-do day a-loo-byas
bean stew

cocido madrileño
ko-thee-do ma-dree-len-yo
meat stew with vegetables

coles de Bruselas
ko-les day broo-say-las
Brussels sprouts

coliflor
ko-lee-flor
cauliflower

compota de manzana
kom-po-ta day man-tha-na
apple compote

conejo con caracoles
ko-ne-ho kon ka-ra-ko-les
rabbit with escargot

conejo estofado
ko-ne-ho e-sto-fa-do
stuffed rabbit

cordero en asador
kor-dair-o en a-sa-dor
mutton on the spit

Menu Reader

dátiles
da-tee-les
dates

en salsa
en sal-sa
in sauce

ensalada
en-sa-la-da
salad

ensalada de maíz
en-sa-la-da day my-eeth
corn salad

ensalada de patata
en-sa-la-da day pa-ta-ta
potato salad

ensalada de pepino
en-sa-la-da day pe-pee-nee-yo
cucumber salad

ensalada de tomate
en-sa-la-da day to-ma-tay
tomato salad

ensalada mixta
en-sa-la-da meek-sta
mixed salad

ensaladilla rusa
en-sa-la-dee-ya roo-sa
Russian salad

escarola
e-ska-ro-la
chicory

espaguetis
es-pa-ge-tees
spaghetti

espárragos
es-pa-ra-gos
asparagus

espinacas
es-pee-na-kas
spinach

estragón
es-tra-gon
tarragon

fabada
fa-ba-da
bean and pork stew

faisán
fy-ee-san
pheasant

filete
fee-le-tay
steak fillet

filete de merluza
fee-le-tay day mair-loo-tha
hake fillet

Menu reader

filete de vaca
fee-le-tay day ba-ka
beefsteak

flan
flan
creme caramel

frambuesas
fram-bway-sas
raspberries

fresas
fray-sas
strawberries

fresas con nata
fray-sas kon na-ta
strawberries with cream

fruta con nata montada
froo-ta kon na-ta
mon-ta-da
fruit with whipped cream

gazpacho
gath-pa-cho
cold soup with cucumber,
tomato, garlic etc

granada
gra-na-da
pomegranate

grosellas negras
gro-se-yas ne-gras
blackcurrants

guisado de carne
gee-sa-do day kar-nay
beef stew

guisado de pollo
gee-sa-do day po-yo
chicken stew

guisantes
gee-san-tes
peas

habas
a-bas
broad beans

helado
e-la-do
ice cream

hierbabuena
yair-ba-bway-na
mint

hoja de laurel
o-ha day low-rel
bayleaf

huevo pasado por agua
way-bo pa-sa-do por a-gwa
soft boiled egg

Menu reader

huevos con jamón
way-bos kon ha-mon
eggs with ham

huevos con tocino
way-bos kon to-thee-no
eggs with bacon

huevos fritos por un lado
way-bos free-tos por oon la-do
eggs sunny side up

huevos revueltos
way-bos re-bwel-tos
scrambled eggs

jamón serrano
ha-mon se-ra-no
cured ham

judías verdes
hoo-dee-as bair-des
French beans

langosta
lan-go-sta
lobster

langostinos rebozados
lan-go-stee-nos re-bo-tha-dos
scampi

lechón en asador
le-chon en a-sa-dor
suckling pig on the spit

lechuga
le-choo-ga
lettuce

lengua
len-gwa
tongue

limón
lee-mon
lemon

macedonia de frutas
ma-the-do-nee-a day froo-tas
fruit salad

maíz
my-eeth
sweet corn

manzana asada
man-tha-na a-sa-da
roast apple

manzanas
man-tha-nas
apples

mejillones
me-hee-yo-nes
mussels

melocotón
me-lo-ko-ton
peach

Menu reader

melón
me-lon
melon

merluza en salsa verde
mair-loo-tha en sal-sa bair-day
hake in parsley sauce

mermelada
mair-me-la-da
jam

morcilla
mor-thee-ya
blood sausage

mousse de chocolate
moos day cho-ko-la-tay
chocolate mousse

nabo
na-bo
turnip

naranjas
na-ran-has
oranges

natillas
na-tee-yas
custard

oca
o-ka
goose

oles de bruselas
cko-les day broo-se-las
Brussels sprouts

ollos de pan
bbo-yos day pan
bread rolls

ostras
o-stras
oysters

ostras fritas
o-stras free-tas
fried oysters (Galicia)

paella
py-e-ya
paella - rice dish

pasta
pa-sta
pasta

patas de rana fritas
pa-tas day ra-na free-tas
fried frog legs

patatas a la riojana
*pa-ta-tas a la
ree-o-ha-na*
potatoes cooked with
tomatoes and
haricot beans (La Rioja)

Menu reader

patatas asadas
pa-ta-tas a-sa-das
roast potatoes

patatas fritas
pa-ta-tas free-tas
French fries

**patatas troceadas y
verdura con mayonesa**
*pa-ta-tas tro-thay-a-das
y bair-doo-ra kon
my-o nay-sa*
cubed potatoes and
vegetables with
mayonnaise

pato
pa-to
duck

**pato relleno con
manzanas**
*pa-to re-yay-no kon
man-tha-nas*
roast duck with apples

pavo
pa-bo
turkey

pepinillo
pe-pee-nee-yo
gherkin

pepino
pe-pee-no
cucumber

pera
pay-ra
pear

perdiz en chocolate
pair-deeth en cho-ko-la-tay
partridge with a
chocolate sauce
(Navarre)

perejil
pe-re-heel
parsley

perifollo
pe-ree-fo-yo
chervil

perrito caliente
pe-ree-to kal-lee-en-tay
hot dog

pescado
pes-ka-do
fish

pescado en escabeche
*pes-ka-do en
es-ka-be-chay*
marinated fish

Menu reader

pierna (de cordero etc)
pee-air-na (day kor-dair-o etc)
shank (of lamb etc)

pimiento rojo
peem-yen-to ro-ho
red pepper

pimiento verde
peem-yen-to bair-day
green pepper

pimientos rellenos
peem-yen-tos re-yay-nos
stuffed peppers

piña
peen-ya
pineapple

plátano
pla-ta-no
banana

pollo cocido/asado
po-yo ko-thee-do/a-sa-do
baked/roasted chicken

pollo frito/rebozado
po-yo free-to/re-bo-tha-do
fried/breaded chicken

pomelo
po-me-lo
grapefruit

puerros
pwe-ros
leeks

puré de patatas
poo-ray day pa-ta-tas
mashed potatoes

queso manchego
ke-so man-chay-go
la Mancha cheese

rábanos
ra-ba-nos
radishes

remolacha
re-mo-la-cha
beetroot

riñones guisados
reen-yo-nes gee-sa-dos
stewed kidney

romero
ro-mair-o
rosemary

rucha cocida
troo-cha ko-thee-da
boiled trout

salchicha
sal-chee-cha
sausage

Menu reader

salmonete
sal-mo-ne-tay
mullet

salsa de cebolla
sal-sa day the-bo-ya
onion sauce

salsa de manzana
sal-sa day man-tha-na
applesauce

salsa de pimiento verde
sal-sa day peem-yen-to
green pepper sauce

salsa de tomate
sal-sa day to-ma-tay
tomato sauce

salsa de vino
sal-sa day bee-no
wine sauce

salvia
sal-bee-a
sage

sandía
san-dee-a
watermelon

sandwich de jamón
san-weech day ha-**mon**
ham sandwich

sandwich frío
san-weech free-o
cold sandwich

sardinas
sar-dee-nas
sardines

sepia
se-pee-a
cuttlefish

sopa de ajo
so-pa day a-ho
garlic soup

sopa de crema de champiñones
so-pa day kray-ma day cham-peen-yo-nes
cream of mushroom soup

sopa de fideos
so-pa day fee-day-os
noodle soup

sopa de frijoles
so-pa day free-ho-les
kidney-bean soup

sopa de guisantes
so-pa day gee-san-tes
pea soup

Menu reader

sopa de pollo
so-pa day po-yo
chicken soup

sopa de puerros
so-pa day pwe-ros
leek soup

sopa de tomate
so-pa day to-ma-tay
tomato soup

tallarines de huevo
ta-ya-ree-nes day way-bo
egg noodles

tarta
tar-ta
cake

tarta
tar-ta
pie

tarta de almendra
tar-ta day al-men-dra
almond cake

tarta de limón
tar-ta day lee-mon
lemon meringue

tarta de manzana
tar-ta day man-tha-na
apple cake

tomates
to-ma-tes
tomatoes

tomillo
to-mee-yo
thyme

tortas
tor-tas
thin pancakes

— con chocolate
— kon cho-ko-la-tay
—with chocolate

— con mermelada
— kon mair-me-la-da
—with jam

tortilla española
tor-tee-ya es-pan-yo-la
Spanish omelette

trucha
troo-cha
trout

trucha frita
troo-cha free-ta
fried trout

uvas
oo-bas
grapes

verduras
bair-doo-ras
vegetables

vinagre
bee-na-gray
vinegar

yogur
yo-goor
yoghurt

zanahoria
tha-na-o-ree-a
carrot

Drinks

agua mineral
a-gwa mee-ne-ral
mineral water

aguardiente
a-gwar-dee-en-tay
brandy

aguardiente de cerezas
a-gwar-dee-en-tay day the-ray-thas
cherry brandy

aguardiente de manzanas
a-gwar-dee-en-tay day man-tha-nas
apple brandy

americano
ka-fay a-me-ree-ka-no
cafe large black coffee

anís
a-nees
anis

cafe con hielo
ka-fay kon ye-lo
iced coffee

cafe escocés
ka-fay es-ko-thes
coffee with whisky and ice cream

cafe instantáneo
ka-fay een-stan-ta-nay-o
instant coffee

cafe irlandés
ka-fay eer-lan-des
Irish coffee

Drinks

cafe sólo
ka-fay so-lo
small black coffee

café
ka-fay
coffee

café con leche
ka-fay kon le-chay
coffee with milk

carajillo
ka-ra-hee-yo
coffee with a dash of brandy

capuchino
ka-poo-chee-no
cappuccino

cerveza
thair-bay-tha
beer

cerveza embotellada
thair-bay-tha em-bo-te-ya-da
bottled beer

cerveza enlatada
thair-bay-tha en-la-ta-da
canned beer

cerveza negra
thair-bay-tha ne-gra
stout

champán
cham-pan
champagne

coca-cola
ko-ka-ko-la
coke

cortado
kor-ta-do
coffee with a dash of milk

descafeinado
des-ka-fay-na-do
decaffeinated coffee

horchata
or-cha-ta
tiger nut milk

licor
lee-kor
liqueur

limonada
lee-mo-na-da
lemonade

manzanilla
man-tha-nee-ya
camomile tea

naranjada
na-ran-ha-da
orange drink

Drinks

pacharán
pa-cha-ran
a type of sloe gin

ron
ron
rum

sangría
san-gree-a
fruit cup with wine

sidra
see-dra
cider

soda
so-da
soda

té
tay
tea

té con leche
tay kon le-chay
tea with milk

té con limón
tay kon lee-mon
lemon tea

tónica
to-nee-ka
tonic water

un coñac
oon kon-yak
a brandy

un vaso de vino blanco
oon ba-so day bee-no blan-ko
a glass of white wine

un vaso de vino tinto
oon ba-so day bee-no teen-to
a glass of red wine

una cerveza grande
oo-na thair-bay-tha gran-day
a large beer

vermut
bair-moot
vermouth

vino rosado
bee-no ro-sa-do
rosé wine

whisky
wee-skee
whisky

zumo de albaricoque
thoo-mo day al-ba-ree-ko-kay
apricot juice

Drinks

zumo de manzana
thoo-mo day man-tha-na
apple juice

zumo de melocotón
thoo-mo day me-lo-ko-ton
peach juice

zumo de naranja
thoo-mo day na-ran-ha
orange juice

zumo de uva
thoo-mo day oo-ba
grape juice

Out and About

The weather

Is it going to get any warmer?
¿Va a hacer más calor?
*ba a a-**thair** mas ka-**lor***

Is it going to stay like this?
¿Va a continuar así?
*ba a kon-tee-**nwar** a-**see***

Is there going to be a thunderstorm?
¿Va a haber tormenta?
*ba a a-**bair** tor-**men**-ta*

Isn't it a lovely day?
¿No es éste un día maravilloso?
*no es es-tay oon **dee**-a ma-ra-bee-yo-so*

It has stopped snowing
Ha parado de nevar
*a pa-**ra**-do day ne-**bar***

It is a very clear night
Hace una noche muy despejada
*a-**thay** oo-na **no**-chay mwee des-pe-**ha**-da*

It is far too hot
Hace demasiado calor
*a-**thay** de-ma-**sya**-do ka-**lor***

It is foggy
Hay niebla
a-ee nee-e-bla

The weather

It is raining again
Está lloviendo de nuevo
es-ta yo-byen-do day nway-bo

It is very cold
Hace mucho frío
a-thay moo-cho free-o

It is very windy
Hace mucho viento
a-thay moo-cho bee-en-to

There is a cool breeze
Hay una brisa fresca
a-ee oo-na bree-sa fre-ska

What is the temperature?
¿Qué temperatura hace?
kay tem-pe-ra-too-ra a-thay

It is going — to be fine
    Va — a hacer bueno
    ba — a a-thair bway-no

      — to be windy
      — a hacer viento
      — a a-thair bee-en-to

      — to rain
      — a llover
      — a yo-bair

      — to snow
      — a nevar
      — a ne-bar

On the beach

Will it be cold tonight?
¿Hará frío esta noche?
a-ra free-o es-ta no-chay

Will the weather improve?
¿Va a mejorar el tiempo?
ba a me-ho-rar el tee-em-po

Will the wind die down?
¿Va a amainar el viento?
ba a a-my-nar el bee-en-to

On the beach

Can we change here?
¿Podemos cambiarnos aquí?
po-day-mos kam-byar-nos a-kee

Can you recommend a quiet beach?
¿Puede sugerir una playa tranquila?
pwe-day soo-he-reer oo-na ply-a tran-kee-la

Is it safe to swim here?
¿Es seguro nadar aquí?
es se-goo-ro na-dar a-kee

Is the current strong?
¿Hay mucha corriente?
a-ee moo-cha ko-ree-en-tay

Is the sea calm?
¿Está la mar tranquila?
es-ta la mar tran-kee-la

On the beach

Can I rent — a sailing boat?
¿Puedo alquilar — un barco de vela?
pwe-do al-kee-lar — oon bar-ko day bay-la

> **— a rowing boat?**
> — un bote de remos?
> — *oon bo-tay day re-mos*

Is it possible to go — sailing?
¿Es posible — salir a navegar?
es po-see-blay — sa-leer a na-be-gar

> **— surfing?**
> — hacer surf?
> — *a-thair soorf*

> **— water skiing?**
> — hacer esquí acuático?
> — *a-thair e-skee a-kwa-tee-ko*

> **— wind surfing?**
> — hacer windsurf?
> — *a-thair ween-soorf*

Is the water warm?
¿Está el agua templada?
es-ta el a-gwa tem-pla-da

Is there a heated swimming pool?
¿Hay alguna piscina climatizada?
a-ee al-goo-na pees-thee-na klee-ma-tee-tha-da

Is there a lifeguard here?
¿Hay algún salvavidas aquí?
a-ee al-goon sal-ba-bee-das a-kee

Is this beach private?
¿Es privada esta playa?
es pree-ba-da es-ta ply-a

When is high tide?
¿Cuándo toca marea alta?
kwan-do to-ka ma-ray-a al-ta

When is low tide?
¿Cuándo toca marea baja?
kwan-do to-ka ma-ray-a ba-ha

Sport and recreation

Can I rent the equipment?
¿Puedo alquilar el material?
pwe-do al-kee-lar el ma-te-ree-al

Can we go riding?
¿Podemos ir a montar a caballo?
po-day-mos eer a mon-tar a ka-ba-yo

    Can we — play tennis?
  ¿Podemos — jugar al tenis?
po-day-mos — hoo-gar al te-nees

        — play golf?
        — jugar al golf?
        — hoo-gar al golf

        — play volleyball?
        — jugar a vóleibol?
        — hoo-gar al bo-lee-bol

Sport and recreation

Where can we fish?
¿Dónde podemos pescar?
don-day po-day-mos pe-skar

Do we need a permit?
¿Necesitamos permiso?
ne-the-see-ta-mos pair-mee-so

Entertainment

How much is it for a child?
¿Cuánto cuesta para un niño?
kwan-to kwe-sta pa-ra oon neen-yo

How much is it per person?
¿Cuánto cuesta por persona?
kwan-to kwe-sta por pair-so-na

How much is it to get in?
¿Cuánto cuesta la entrada?
kwan-to kwe-sta la en-tra-da

Is there — a disco?
  ¿Hay — alguna discoteca?
  a-ee — al-goo-na dee-sko-tay-ka

> **— a good nightclub?**
> — algún buen club?
> *— al-goon bwen kloob*

> **— a theatre?**
> — teatro?
> *— tay-a-tro*

Sightseeing

Are there any films in English?
¿Hay alguna película en inglés?
a-ee al-goo-na pe-lee-koo-la en een-gles

Two stall tickets, please
Dos entradas en butacas, por favor
dos en-tra-das en boo-ta-kas, por fa-bor

Two tickets, please
Dos entradas, por favor
dos en-tra-das, por fa-bor

Is there a reduction for children?
¿Hay descuento para niños?
a-ee des-kwen-to pa-ra neen-yos

Sightseeing

Are there any boat trips on the river?
¿Hay excursiones en barco por el río?
a-ee ek-skoor-syo-nes en bar-ko por el ree-o

Are there any guided tours of the castle?
¿Hay alguna visita con guía al castillo?
a-ee al-goo-na bee-see-ta kon gee-a al ka-stee-yo

Are there any guided tours?
¿Hay visitas con guía?
a-ee bee-see-tas kon gee-a

What is there to see here?
¿Qué hay para ver aquí?
kay a-ee pa-ra bair a-kee

Sightseeing

What is this building?
¿Qué es este edificio?
kay es es-tay e-dee-fee-thee-o

When was it built?
¿Cuándo se construyó?
kwan-do say kon-stroo-yo

Is it open to the public?
¿Está abierto al público?
es-ta a-bee-air-to al poo-blee-ko

What is the admission charge?
¿Cuánto cuesta la entrada?
kwan-to kwes-ta la en-tra-da

Can we go in?
¿Podemos entrar?
po-day-mos en-trar

Can we go up to the top?
¿Podemos subir hasta arriba?
po-day-mos soo-beer a-sta a-ree-ba

Can I take photos?
¿Puedo hacer fotos?
pwe-do a-thair fo-tos

Can I use flash?
¿Puedo utilizar flash?
pwe-do oo-tee-lee-thar flas

How long does the tour take?
¿Cuánto dura la excursión?
kwan-to doo-ra la ek-skoor-syon

Souvenirs

Is there a guide book?
¿Hay alguna guía turística?
a-ee al-goo-na gee-a too-ree-stee-ka

Is there a tour of the cathedral?
¿Hay visita a la catedral?
a-ee bee-see-ta a la ka-te-dral

Is there an English-speaking guide?
¿Hay algún guía que hable inglés?
a-ee al-goon gee-a kay a-blay een-gles

Is this the best view?
¿Es ésta la mejor vista?
es es-ta la me-hor bee-sta

What time does the gallery open?
¿A qué hora abre la galería?
a kay o-ra a-bray la ga-le-ree-a

When is the bus tour?
¿Cuándo es la visita en autobús?
kwan-do es la bee-see-ta en ow-to-boos

Souvenirs

Have you got an English guidebook?
¿Tiene alguna guía turística en inglés?
tee-e-nay al-goo-na gee-a too-ree-stee-ka en een-gles

Have you got any colour slides?
¿Tiene diapositivas en color?
tee-e-nay dee-a-po-zee-tee-bas en ko-lor

Souvenirs

Where can I buy postcards?
¿Dónde puedo comprar postales?
don-day pwe-do kom-prar po-sta-les

Where can we buy souvenirs?
¿Dónde podemos comprar recuerdos?
don-day po-day-mos kom-prar re-kwair-dos

Going to church

Where is the	**— Catholic church?**
¿Dónde está la	— iglesia Católica?
don-day es-ta la	*— ee-glay-see-a ka-to-lee-ka*

— Baptist church?
— la iglesia Bautista?
— la ee-glay-see-a bow-tee-sta

— mosque?
— la mezquita?
— la meth-kee-ta

— Protestant church?
— iglesia Protestante?
— ee-glay-see-a pro-te-stan-tay

— synagogue?
— la sinagoga?
— la see-na-go-ga

What time is the service?
¿A qué hora es la misa?
a kay o-ra es la mee-sa

Going to church

I would like to see — a priest
Me gustaría hablar con — un sacerdote
*may goo-sta-**ree**-a a-**blar** kon — oon sa-**thair**-**do**-tay*

— a minister
— un pastor
*— oon pa-**stor***

— a rabbi
— un rabino
*— oon ra-**bee**-no*

SHOPPING

General phrases and requests

How much does that cost?
¿Cuánto cuesta eso?
kwan-to kwes-ta e-so

How much is it — per kilo?
¿Cuánto cuesta — por kilo?
kwan-to kwes-ta — por kee-lo

        — per metre?
        — por metro?
        — por me-tro

How much is this?
¿Cuánto es esto?
kwan-to es es-to

Have you got anything cheaper?
¿Tiene algo más barato?
tee-e-nay al-go mas ba-ra-to

Can I see that umbrella?
¿Puedo ver ese paraguas?
pwe-do bair e-say pa-ra-gwas

No, the other one
No, el otro
no, el o-tro

Can you deliver to my hotel?
¿Puede entregármelo al hotel?
pwe-day en-tre-gar-may-lo al o-tel

General phrases and requests

I do not like it
No me gusta
no may goo-sta

I like this one
Me gusta éste
may goo-sta es-tay

I will take — this one
   Tomaré — éste
to-ma-ray — es-tay

       — that one
       — ése
       — e-say

       — the other one
       — el otro
       — el o-tro

       — that one over there
       — aquél de allí
       — a-kel day a-ye

Where can I buy some clothes?
¿Dónde puedo comprar ropa?
don-day pwe-do kom-prar ro-pa

Where can I buy tapes for my camcorder?
¿Dónde puedo comprar cintas para el camcórder?
don-day pwe-do kom-prar theen-tas pa-ra el kam-kor-dair

Where can I get my camcorder repaired?
¿A dónde puedo llevar a reparar el camcórder?
a don-day pwe-do ye-bar a re-pa-rar el kam-kor-dair

General phrases and requests

Where is — the children's department?
¿Dónde está — el departamento infantil?
don-day es-ta — el de-par-ta-men-to een-fan-teel

— the food department?
— el departamento de comestibles?
— el de-par-ta-men-to day ko-me-stee-blays

I am looking for a souvenir
Estoy buscando un recuerdo
es-toy boo-skan-do oon re-kwair-do

Do you sell sunglasses?
¿Venden gafas de sol?
ben-den ga-fas day sol

Can I have — a carrier bag?
¿Puede darme — una bolsa?
pwe-day dar-may — oo-na bol-sa

— a receipt?
— un recibo?
— oon re-thee-bo

— an itemised bill?
— una cuenta detallada?
— oo-na kwen-ta de-ta-ya-da

Can I pay for air insurance?
¿Puedo pagar un seguro aéreo?
pwe-do pa-gar oon se-goo-ro a-air-ay-o

What is the total?
¿Cuánto es el total?
kwan-to es el to-tal

General phrases and requests

Do you accept traveller's cheques?
¿Acepta cheques de viaje?
*a-**thep**-ta **che**-kays day bee-a-hay*

I do not have enough currency
No tengo suficiente cambio
*no **ten**-go soo-fee-**thyen**-tay **kam**-bee-o*

I do not have enough money
No tengo suficiente dinero
*no **ten**-go soo-fee-**thyen**-tay dee-**ne**-o*

I would like to pay with my credit card
Me gustaría pagar con tarjeta de crédito
*may goo-sta-**ree**-a pa-**gar** kon tar-**hay**-ta day **kre**-dee-t*

Please forward a receipt to this address
Por favor, envíe un recibo a esta dirección
*por fa-**bor**, en-bee-ay oon re-**thee**-bo a es-ta dee-rek-**thyon**

Please wrap it up for me
Por favor, envuélvamelo
*por fa-**bor**, en-**bwel**-ba-may-lo*

There is no need to wrap it
No hace falta envolverlo
*no **a-thay** fal-ta en-bol-**bair**-lo*

Please pack this for shipment
Por favor, envuelva esto para envía
*por fa-**bor**, en-**bwel**-ba es-to pa-ra en-**bee**-o*

Will you send it by air freight?
¿Lo enviará por avión?
*lo en-bee-a-**ra** por a-**byon***

Buying groceries

We need to buy some food
Tenemos que comprar comida
te-nay-mos kay kom-prar ko-mee-da

I would like — a kilo of potatoes
Me da — un kilo de patatas
may da — oon kee-lo day pa-ta-tas

— a bar of chocolate
— una barra de chocolate
— oo-na ba-ra day cho-ko-la-tay

— 100 g of ground coffee
— cien gramos de café molido
— thee-en gra-mos day ka-fay mo-lee-do

— two steaks
— dos filetes
— dos fee-le-tes

— 5 slices of ham
— cinco lonchas de jamón
— theen-ko lon-chas day ha-mon

— half a dozen eggs
— media docena de huevos
— me-dee-a do-thay-na day way-bos

— half a kilo of butter
— medio kilo de mantequilla
— me-dee-o kee-lo day man-te-kee-ya

Groceries

Can I have — some sugar, please?
¿Puede darme — azúcar, por favor?
pwe-day dar-may — a-thoo-kar, por fa-bor

— **a bottle of wine, please?**
— una botella de vino , por favor?
— *oo-na bo-te-ya day bee-no, por fa-bor*

— **a kilo of sausages, please?**
— un kilo de salchichas, por favor?
— *oon kee-lo day sal-chee-chas, por fa-bor*

— **a leg of lamb, please?**
— una pierna de cordero, por favor?
— *oo-na pee-air-na day kor-dair-o, por fa-bor*

— **a litre of milk, please?**
— un litro de leche, por favor?
— *oon lee-tro day le-chay, por fa-bor*

Groceries

baby food	**butter**
comida para bebés	mantequilla
ko-mee-da pa-ra be-bes	*man-te-kee-ya*
biscuits	**cheese**
galletas	queso
ga-yay-tas	*ke-so*
bread	**coffee**
pan	café
pan	*ka-fay*

Groceries

cream nata *na-ta*	**pepper** pimienta *peem-yen-ta*
eggs huevos *way-bos*	**rice** arroz *a-roth*
flour harina *a-ree-na*	**salt** sal *sal*
jam mermelada *mair-me-la-da*	**soup** sopa *so-pa*
margarine margarina *mar-ga-ree-na*	**sugar** azúcar *a-thoo-kar*
milk leche *le-chay*	**tea** té *tay*
mustard mostaza *mo-sta-tha*	**vinegar** vinagre *bee-na-gray*
oil aceite *a-thay-ee-tay*	**yoghurt** yogur *yo-goor*

Meat and fish

beef
vaca
_ba-ka_

chicken
pollo
_po-yo_

cod
bacalao
_ba-ka-la-o_

fish
pescado
pe-ska-do

ham
jamón
ha-mon

herring
arenque
a-ren-kay

kidneys
riñones
reen-yo-nes

lamb
cordero
kor-dair-o

liver
hígado
_ee-ga-do_

meat
carne
kar-nay

mussels
mejillones
me-hee-yo-nes

pork
cerdo
thair-do

sole
lenguado
len-gwa-do

veal
ternera
tair-nair-a

At the newsagent's

Do you sell — English paperbacks?
   ¿Vende — libros de bolsillo en inglés?
   ben-day — lee-bros day bol-see-yo en een-gles

   — postcards?
   — postales?
   — po-sta-les

   — a local map?
   — un plano de la localidad?
   — oon pla-no day la lo-ka-lee-dad

   — a road map?
   — un mapa de carreteras?
   — oon ma-pa day ka-re-tair-as

   — coloured pencils?
   — lápices de color?
   — la-pee-thes day ko-lor

   — drawing paper?
   — papel de dibujo?
   — pa-pel day dee-boo-ho

   — felt pens?
   — rotuladores?
   — ro-too-la-do-res

   — street maps?
   — planos de ciudad?
   — pla-nos day thee-oo-dad

At the newsagent's

I would like some postage stamps
Me da sellos de correos
may da se-yos day ko-ray-os

Do you have — English books?
¿Tiene — libros en inglés?
tee-e-nay — lee-bros en een-gles

— English newspapers?
— periódicos en inglés?
— pe-ree-o-dee-kos en een-gles

I need — some note paper
Necesito — papel de cartas
ne-the-see-to — pa-pel day kar-tas

— a bottle of ink
— una botella de tinta
— oo-na bo-te-ya day teen-ta

— a pen
— un bolígrafo
— oon bo-lee-gra-fo

— a pencil
— un lápiz
— oon la-peeth

— some adhesive tape
— cinta adhesiva
— theen-ta a-de-see-ba

— some envelopes
— sobres
— so-bres

At the tobacconist's

Do you have — cigarette papers?
   ¿Tiene — papel de fumar?
   *tee-e-nay — pa-**pel** day foo-**mar***

   — a box of matches
   — una caja de cerillas
   — *oo-na **ka**-ha day the-**ree**-yas*

   — a cigar
   — un cigarro
   — *oon thee-**ga**-ro*

   — a cigarette lighter
   — un mechero
   — *oon me-**chair**-o*

   — a gas (butane) refill
   — una carga de gas
   — *oo-na **kar**-ga day gas*

   — a pipe
   — una pipa
   — *oo-na **pee**-pa*

   — a pouch of pipe tobacco
   — una petaca de tabaco de pipa
   — *oo-na pe-**ta**-ka day ta-**ba**-ko day **pee**-pa*

   — some pipe cleaners
   — unos limpiapipas
   — *oo-nos leem-pya-**pee**-pas*

Have you got — any American brands?
   ¿Tiene — marcas americanas?
   tee-e-nay — mar-kas a-me-ree-ka-nas

                 — any English brands?
                 — marcas inglesas?
                 — mar-kas een-glay-sas

                 — rolling tobacco?
                 — tabaco de liar?
                 — ta-ba-ko day lee-ar

A packet of ... please
Un paquete de ... por favor
oon pa-ke-tay day ... por fa-bor

— with filter tips
— con filtro
— kon feel-tro

— without filters
— sin filtro
— seen feel-tro

At the chemist's

Do you have toothpaste?
¿Tiene pasta de dientes?
tee-e-nay pa-sta day dee-en-tes

I need some high-protection suntan cream
Necesito una crema solar de alta protección
ne-the-see-to oo-na kray-ma so-lar day al-ta pro-tek-thyon

At the chemist's

Can you give me something for — a headache?
¿Puede darme algo para — el dolor de cabeza?
pwe-day dar-may al-go pa-ra — el do-lor day ka-bay-tha

— **insect bites**
— las picaduras de insectos?
— *las pee-ka-doo-ras day een-sek-tos*

— **a cold**
— un catarro
— *oon ka-ta-ro*

— **a cough**
— tos
— *tos*

— **a sore throat**
— dolor de garganta
— *do-lor day gar-gan-ta*

— **an upset stomach**
— mal del estómago
— *mal day e-sto-ma-go*

— **toothache**
— dolor de muelas
— *do-lor day mway-las*

— **hay fever**
— fiebre del heno
— *fee-e-bray del ay-no*

— **sunburn**
— quemadura de sol
— *ke-ma-doo-ra day sol*

Medicines and toiletries

Do I need a prescription?
¿Necesito una receta?
ne-the-see-to oo-na re-thay-ta

How many do I take?
¿Cuántas tengo que tomar?
kwan-tas ten-go kay to-mar

How often do I take them?
¿Con qué frecuencia tengo que tomarlas?
kon kay fre-kwen-thee-a ten-go kay to-mar-las

Are they safe for children to take?
¿Los niños pueden tomarlas sin riesgo?
los neen-yos pwe-den to-mar-las seen ree-ez-go

Medicines and toiletries

antihistamine
antihistamínico
an-tee-ee-sta-mee-nee-ko

antiseptic
antiséptico
an-tee-sep-tee-ko

aspirin
aspirina
a-spee-ree-na

band-aid
tirita
tee-ree-ta

bandage
vendaje
ben-da-hay

bubble bath
espuma de baño
e-spoo-ma day ban-yo

cleansing milk
leche limpiadora
le-chay leem-pya-do-ra

contraceptive
preservativo
an-tee-kon-thep-tee-bo

Medicines and toiletries

cotton wool
algodón hidrófilo
*al-go-**don** ee-**dro**-fee-lo*

deodorant
desodorante
*des-o-do-**ran**-tay*

disinfectant
desinfectante
*des-een-fek-**tan**-tay*

eau de Cologne
agua de colonia
*a-gwa day ko-**lon**-ya*

eye shadow
sombra de ojos
som-bra day o-hos

hair spray
laca para el cabello
la-ka pa-ra el ka-be-yo

hand cream
crema de manos
kray-ma day ma-nos

insect repellent
insecticida
*een-sek-tee-**thee**-da*

kleenex
kleenex
klee-neks

laxative
laxante
*lak-**san**-tay*

lipstick
barra de labios
ba-ra day la-bee-os

mascara
rímel
ree-mel

mouthwash
antiséptico bucal
*an-tee-**sep**-tee-ko boo-**kal***

nail file
lima de uñas
lee-ma day oon-yas

nail varnish
esmalte de uñas
*es-**mal**-tay day oon-yas*

nail varnish remover
quitaesmalte
*kee-ta-es-**mal**-tay*

perfume
perfume
*pair-**foo**-may*

powder
polvos
pol-bos

Shopping for clothes

razor blades
hojas de afeitar
o-has day a-fay-tar

soap
jabón
ha-bon

sanitary towels
compresas
kom-pray-sas

suntan oil
bronceador
bron-thay-a-dor

shampoo
champú
cham-poo

talc
talco
tal-ko

shaving cream
espuma de afeitar
es-poo-ma day a-fay-tar

toilet water
colonia
ko-lon-ya

skin moisturiser
loción hidratante
lo-thyon ee-dra-tan-tay

toothpaste
pasta de dientes
pa-sta day dee-en-tes

Shopping for clothes

I am just looking, thank you
Sólo estoy mirando, gracias
so-lo es-toy mee-ran-do, gra-thee-as

I do not like it
No me gusta
no may goo-sta

I like it
Me gusta
may goo-sta

Shopping for clothes

I will take it
Lo llevaré
lo ye-ba-ray

I like — this one
Me gusta — éste
may goo-sta — es-tay

— that one there
— aquél
— a-kel

— the one in the window
— el que está en el escaparate
— el kay es-ta en el e-ska-pa-ra-tay

I would like — this suit
Quiero comprar — este traje
kee-e-ro kom-prar — es-tay tra-hay

— this hat
— este sombrero
— es-tay som-brair-o

I would like one — with a zip
Quisiera uno — con cremallera
ke-see-air-a oo-no — kon kre-ma-yair-a

— without a belt
— sin cinturón
— seen then-too-ron

Can you please measure me?
¿Puede medirme, por favor?
pwe-day me-deer-may, por fa-bor

Shopping for clothes

Can I change it if it does not fit?
¿Puedo cambiarlo si no me vale?
pwe-do kam-byar-lo see no may ba-lay

Have you got this in other colours?
¿Tiene éste en otros colores?
tee-e-nay es-tay en o-tros ko-lo-res

I take a large shoe size
Uso una talla de zapato grande
oo-so oo-na ta-ya day tha-pa-to gran-day

I take continental size 40
Uso la talla cuarenta europea
oo-so la ta-ya kwa-ren-ta ay-oo-ro-pay-a

Is it too long?
¿Es demasiado largo?
es de-ma-sya-do lar-go

Is it too short?
¿Es demasiado corto?
es de-ma-sya-do kor-to

Is there a full length mirror?
¿Hay algún espejo de cuerpo entero?
a-ee al-goon es-pe-ho day kwair-po en-tair-o

Is this all you have?
¿Es esto todo lo que tiene?
es es-to to-do lo kay tee-e-nay

It does not fit
No me vale
no may ba-lay

Shopping for clothes

It does not suit me
No me queda bien
*no may **kay**-da byen*

May I see it in daylight?
¿Puedo verlo a la luz del día?
*pwe-do **bair**-lo a la looth del **dee**-a*

Where are the changing (dressing) rooms?
¿Dónde están los probadores?
***don**-day es-**tan** los pro-ba-**do**-res*

Where can I try it on?
¿Dónde puedo probármelo?
***don**-day pwe-do pro-**bar**-may-lo*

Have you got — a large size?
　　　¿Tiene — una talla grande?
　　*tee-e-nay — **oo**-na ta-ya gran-day*

　　　　　— a small size?
　　　　　— una talla pequeña?
　　　　　*— **oo**-na ta-ya pe-**ken**-ya*

What is it made of?
¿De qué material es?
*day kay ma-te-ree-**al** es*

Is it guaranteed?
¿Tiene garantía?
*tee-e-nay ga-ran-**tee**-a*

Will it shrink?
¿Encogerá?
*en-ko-hair-**a***

Clothes and accessories

Is it drip-dry?
¿Es de lava y pon?
es day la-ba ee pon

Is it dry-clean only?
¿Es de limpiar en seco sólamente?
es day leem-pyar en se-ko so-la-men-tay

Is it machine washable?
¿Es lavable a máquina?
es la-ba-blay a ma-kee-na

Clothes and accessories

acrylic
acrílico
a-kree-lee-ko

belt
cinturón
then-too-ron

blouse
blusa
bloo-sa

bra
sujetador
soo-he-ta-dor

bracelet
pulsera
pool-say-ra

brooch
broche
bro-chay

button
botón
bo-ton

cardigan
rebeca
re-bay-ka

coat
abrigo
a-bree-go

corduroy
pana
pa-na

Clothes and accessories

denim
tela vaquera
tay-la ba-kair-a

jacket
cazadora
ka-tha-do-ra

dress
vestido
be-stee-do

jeans
vaqueros
ba-kair-os

dungarees
pantalón de peto
pan-ta-lon day pay-to

jersey
jersey
hair-say

earrings
pendientes
pen-dee-en-tes

lace
encaje
en-ka-hay

fur
piel
pyel

leather
cuero
kwair-o

gloves
guantes
gwan-tes

linen
lino
lee-no

handbag
bolso
bol-so

necklace
collar
ko-yar

handkerchief
pañuelo
pan-yoo-ay-lo

nightdress
camisón
ka-mee-son

hat
sombrero
som-brair-o

nylon
nylon
nee-lon

Clothes and accessories

panties
bragas
bra-gas

pendant
medallón
me-da-yon

petticoat
combinación
kom-bee-na-thyon

polyester
poliéster
po-lee-e-stair

poplin
popelín
po-pe-leen

pullover
pulóver
poo-lo-bair

purse
monedero
mo-ne-dair-o

pyjamas
pijama
pee-ha-ma

raincoat
impermeable
eem-pair-may-a-blay

rayon
rayón
ra-yon

ring
anillo
a-nee-yo

sandals
sandalias
san-da-lee-as

scarf
bufanda
boo-fan-da

shirt
camisa
ka-mee-sa

shorts
pantalón corto
pan-ta-lon kor-to

silk
seda
say-da

skirt
falda
fal-da

slip
enagua
e-na-gwa

Clothes and accessories

socks
calcetines
kal-the-tee-nes

stockings
medias
me-dee-as

suede
ante
an-tay

suit (men's)
traje
tra-hay

suit (women's)
traje de chaqueta
tra-hay day cha-kay-ta

sweater
suéter
swe-tair

swimming trunks
bañador
ban-ya-dor

swimsuit
traje de baño
tra-hay day ban-yo

t-shirt
camiseta
ka-mee-say-ta

terylene
terylene
te-ree-le-nay

tie
corbata
kor-ba-ta

tights
medias
me-dee-as

towel
toalla
to-a-ya

trousers
pantalón
pan-ta-lon

umbrella
paraguas
pa-ra-gwas

underpants
calzoncillos
kal-thon-thee-yos

velvet
terciopelo
tair-thee-o-pe-lo

vest
camiseta
ka-mee-say-ta

Photography

wallet	**wool**
cartera	lana
*kar-**tair**-a*	***la**-na*
watch	**zip**
reloj	cremallera
*re-**loh***	*kre-ma-**yair**-a*

Photography

I need a film — for this camera
Quiero una película — para esta cámara
*kee-e-ro **oo**-na pe-**lee**-koo-la — pa-ra es-ta **ka**-ma-ra*

— for this camcorder
— para esta camcórder
*— pa-ra es-ta kam-**kor**-dair*

— for this cine camera
— para esta cámara de cine
*— pa-ra es-ta ka-ma-ra day **thee**-nay*

— for this video camera
— para este videocámara
*— pa-ra es-tay bee-day-o-**ka**-ma-ra*

Can you develop this film, please?
¿Puede revelar esta película, por favor?
*pwe-day re-be-**lar** es-ta pe-**lee**-koo-la, por fa-**bor***

I would like this photo enlarged
Quiero que amplien esta foto
*kee-e-ro kay am-**plee**-en es-ta **fo**-to*

Photography

I would like two prints of this one
Quiero dos copias de ésta
ke-e-ro dos ko-pyas day es-ta

When will the photos be ready?
¿Cuándo estarán las fotos?
kwan-do es-ta-ran las fo-tos

I want — a black and white film
Quiero — una película en blanco y negro
kee-e-ro— oo-na pe-lee-koo-la en blan-ko ee ne-gro

> **— a colour print film**
> — una película en color
> *— oo-na pe-lee-koo-la en ko-lor*

> **— a colour slide film**
> — una película de diapositivas en color
> *— oo-na pe-lee-koo-la day dee-a-po-zee-tee-bas en ko-lor*

> **— batteries for the flash**
> *— pilas para el flash*
> *— pee-las pa-ra el flas*

Camera repairs

I am having trouble with my camera
Tengo un problema con la cámara
ten-go oon pro-blay-ma kon la ka-ma-ra

The film is jammed
La película está atascada
la pe-lee-koo-la es-ta a-ta-ska-da

Camera parts

There is something wrong with my camera
Le ocurre algo a mi cámara
lay o-koo-ray al-go a mee ka-ma-ra

Where can I get my camera repaired?
¿Dónde puedo llevar la cámara a reparar?
don-day pwe-do ye-bar la ka-ma-ra a re-pa-rar

Camera parts

accessory
accesorio
ak-the-so-ree-o

blue filter
filtro azul
feel-tro a-thool

camcorder
camcórder
kam-kor-dair

cartridge
carrete
ka-re-tay

cassette
cassette
ka-se-tay

cine camera
cámara de cine
ka-ma-ra day thee-nay

distance
distancia
dee-stan-thee-a

enlargement
ampliación
am-plee-a-thyon

exposure
exposición
ek-spo-zee-thyon

exposure meter
fotómetro
fo-to-me-tro

flash bulb
bombilla de flash
bom-bee-ya day flas

flash cube
cubo de flash
koo-bo day flas

Camera parts

flash
flash
flas

focal distance
distancia focal
dee-stan-thee-a fo-kal

focus
foco
fo-ko

image
imagen
ee-ma-hen

in focus
enfocado
en-fo-ka-do

lens cover
tapa de objetivo
ta-pa day ob-he-tee-bo

lens
objetivo
ob-he-tee-bo

negative
negativo
ne-ga-tee-bo

out of focus
desenfocado
des-en-fo-ka-do

over exposed
sobrexpuesto
so-bray-eks-pwes-to

picture
fotografía
fo-to-gra-fee-a

print
copia
ko-pya

projector
proyector
pro-yek-tor

red filter
filtro rojo
feel-tro ro-ho

reel
rollo
ro-yo

shade
sombra
som-bra

shutter
obturador
ob-too-ra-dor

shutter speed
velocidad de obturación
be-lo-thee-dad day ob-too-ra-thyon

At the hairdresser's

slide
diapositiva
dee-a-po-zee-tee-ba

transparency
transparencia
trans-pa-ren-thee-a

tripod
trípode
tree-po-day

viewfinder
visor
bee-sor

wide angle lens
granangular
gra-nan-goo-lar

yellow filter
filtro amarillo
feel-tro a-ma-ree-yo

At the hairdresser's

I would like to make an appointment
Quisiera reservar hora
kee-see-air-a re-sair-bar o-ra

I want — a haircut
Quiero — cortarme el pelo
kee-e-ro — kor-tar-may el pelo

      — a trim
      — cortarme las puntas
      — kor-tar-may las poon-tas

Not too much off
No quite demasiado
no kee-tay de-ma-sya-do

Take a little more off the back
Quite un poco más por detrás
kee-tay oon po-ko mas por de-tras

At the hairdresser's

Please cut my hair — short
Por favor, córteme el pelo — corto
*por fa-**bor**, **kor**-tay-may el **pe**-lo — **kor**-to*

— fairly short
— bastante corto
*— ba-**stan**-tay **kor**-to*

— in a fringe
— con flequillo
*— kon fle-**kee**-yo*

That is fine, thank you
Está bien, gracias
*es-ta byen, **gra**-thee-as*

I would like — a perm
Quisiera — una permanente
*kee-see-**air**-ra — **oo**-na pair-ma-**nen**-tay*

— a blow-dry
— secar con secador
*— se-**kar** kon se-ka-**dor***

— my hair dyed
— teñirme el pelo
*— ten-**yeer**-may el **pe**-lo*

— my hair streaked
— mechas en el pelo
*— **may**-chas en el **pe**-lo*

— shampoo and cut
— lavar y cortar
*— la-**bar** ee kor-**tar***

Laundry

I would like — shampoo and set
   Quisiera — lavar y marcar
kee-see-air-ra — la-bar e mar-kar

> **— a conditioner**
> — un suavizante
> *— oon swa-bee-than-tay*

> **— hair spray**
> — laca de pelo
> *— la-ka day pe-l*

The dryer is too hot
El secador está demasiado caliente
el se-ka-dor es-ta de-ma-sya-do ka-lee-en-tay

The water is too hot
El agua está demasiado caliente
el a-gwa es-ta de-ma-sya-do ka-lee-en-tay

Laundry

Is there a launderette nearby?
¿Hay alguna lavandería cercana?
a-ee al-goo-na la-ban-de-ree-a thair-ka-na

How does the washing machine work?
¿Cómo funciona la lavadora?
ko-mo foon-thyo-na la la-ba-do-ra

How long will it take?
¿Cuánto tardará?
kwan-to tar-da-ra

Laundry

Can you — clean this skirt?
¿Me puede — limpiar esta falda?
may pwe-day — leem-pyar es-ta fal-da

— clean and press these shirts?
— limpiar y planchar estas camisas?
— leem-pyar ee plan-char es-tas ka-mee-sas

— wash these clothes?
— lavar esta ropa?
— la-bar es-ta ro-pa

This stain is — oil
Esta mancha es — de aceite
es-ta man-cha es — day a-thay-ee-tay

— blood
— de sangre
— day san-gray

— coffee
— de café
— day ka-fay

— ink
— de tinta
— day teen-ta

This fabric is delicate
Esta tela es delicada
es-ta tay-la es de-lee-ka-da

I have lost my dry cleaning ticket
He perdido el resguardo de la tintorería
ay pair-dee-do el rez-gwar-do day la teen-to-re-ree-a

General repairs

Please send it to this address
Por favor, envíelo a esta dirección
por fa-bor, en-bee-ay-lo a es-ta dee-rek-thyon

When will I come back?
¿Cuándo puedo volver?
kwan-do pwe-do bol-bair

When will my clothes be ready?
¿Cuándo estará mi ropa lista?
kwan-do es-ta-ra mee ro-pa lee-sta

I will come back — later
Volveré — más tarde
bol-bair-ay — mas tar-day

— in an hour
— dentro de una hora
— den-tro day oo-na o-ra

General repairs

This is — broken
Esto está — roto
es-to es-ta — ro-to

— damaged
— averiado
— a-be-ree-a-do

— torn
— estropeado
— e-stro-pay-a-do

General repairs

Can you repair it?
¿Puede repararlo?
pwe-day re-pa-rar-lo

Can you do it quickly?
¿Puede hacerlo rápidamente?
pwe-day a-thair-lo ra-pee-da-men-tay

Have you got a spare part for this?
¿Tiene alguna pieza de repuesto para esto?
tee-e-nay al-goo-na pee-ay-tha day re-pwe-sto pa-ra es-to

Would you have a look at this please?
¿Puede mirar esto, por favor?
pwe-day mee-rar es-to, por fa-bor

Here is the guarantee
Aquí está la garantía
a-kee es-ta la ga-ran-tee-aWhat' wrong

At the Post Office

12 stamps please
Doce sellos, por favor
do-thay se-yos, por fa-bor

I need to send this by courier
Necesito enviar esto por servicio de mensajero
ne-the-see-to en-byar esto por sair-bee-thee-o day men-sa-hair-o

I want to send a telegram
Quiero enviar este telegrama
kee-e-ro en-byar es-tay te-le-gra-ma

At the Post Office

I want to send this by registered mail
Quiero enviar esto por correo certificado
kee-e-ro en-byar es-to por ko-ray-o thair-tee-fee-ka-do

I want to send this parcel
Quiero enviar este paquete
kee-e-ro en-byar es-tay pa-ke-tay

When will it arrive?
¿Cuándo llegará?
kwan-do ye-ga-ra

How much is a letter — to Britain?
¿Cuánto cuesta una carta — a Gran Bretaña?
kwan-to kwes-ta oo-na kar-ta — a gran bre-tan-ya

— to the United States?
— a los Estados Unidos?
— a los e-sta-dos oo-nee-dos

Can I have six stamps for postcards to Britain?
Me da seis sellos para postales a Gran Bretaña
may da says se-yos pa-ra po-sta-les a gran bre-tan-ya

Can I have a telegram form, please?
¿Puede darme un impreso de telegrama, por favor?
pwe-day dar-may oon eem-pray-so day te-le-gra-ma, por fa-bor

Using the telephone

Can I use the telephone, please?
¿Puedo utilizar el teléfono, por favor?
pwe-do oo-tee-lee-thar el te-le-fo-no, por fa-bor

Can I dial direct?
¿Puedo marcar directamente?
pwe-do mar-kar dee-rek-ta-men-tay

Can you connect me with the international operator?
¿Puede conectarme con la operador a internacional?
pwe-day ko-nek-tar-may kon la o-pe-ra-do-ra een-tair-na-thyo-nal

Have you got any change?
¿Tiene cambio?
tee-e-nay kam-bee-o

How do I use the telephone?
¿Cómo se utiliza el teléfono?
ko-mo say oo-tee-lee-tha el te-le-fo-no

How much is it to phone to London?
¿Cuánto cuesta llamar a Londres?
kwan-to kwes-ta ya-mar a lon-dres

I must make a phone call to Britain
Tengo que llamar a Gran Bretaña
ten-go kay ya-mar a gran bre-tan-ya

I need to make a phone call
Tengo que hacer una llamada
ten-go kay a-thair oo-na ya-ma-da

Using the telephone

What is the code for the UK?
¿Cuál es el código del Reino Unido?
kwal es el ko-dee-go del ray-no oo-nee-do

I would like to make a reversed charge call
Deseo hacer una llamada a cobro revertido
de-say-o a-thair oo-na ya-ma-da a ko-bro re-bair-tee-do

The number I need is...
El número que necesito es...
el noo-me-o kay ne-the-see-to es...

What is the charge?
¿Cuánto es?
kwan-to es

Please, call me back
Por favor, devuelva mi llamada
por fa-bor, de-bwel-ba mee ya-ma-da

I am sorry. We were cut off
Lo siento. Se ha cortado
lo syen-to. Say a kor-ta-do

El número no funciona
el noo-me-ro no foon-thyo-na
The number is out of order

Está comunicando
es-ta ko-moo-nee-kan-do
The line is engaged (busy)

Estoy intentando conectarle
es-toy een-ten-tan-do ko-nek-tar-lay
I am trying to connect you

Using the telephone

Hable, por favor
a-blay, por fa-bor
Please go ahead

Hola, soy el director
o-la, soy el dee-rek-tor
Hello, this is the manager

Le voy a pasar con el señor Smith
lay boy a pa-sar kon el sen-yor Smith
I am putting you through to Mr Smith

No puedo obtener este número
no pwe-do ob-te-nair es-tay noo-me-ro
I cannot obtain this number

Changing money

Can I contact my bank to arrange for a transfer?
¿Puedo contactar a mi banco para pedir una
transferencia?
*pwe-do kon-tak-tar a mee ban-ko pa-ra pe-deer oo-na trans-
fe-ren-thee-a*

Has my cash arrived?
¿Ha llegado mi dinero?
a ye-ga-do mee dee-ne-ro

**I would like to obtain a cash advance with my credit
card**
Quisiera un anticipo en metálico con mi tarjeta de crédito
*kee-see-air-ra oon an-tee-thee-po en me-ta-lee-ko kon mee
tar-hay-ta day kre-dee-to*

Changing money

This is the name and address of my bank
Éste es el nombre y la dirección de mi banco
es-ta es el nom-bray ee la dee-rek-thyon day mee ban-ko

   Can I change — these traveller's cheques?
  ¿Puedo cambiar — estos cheques de viaje?
pwe-do kam-byar — es-tos che-kays day bee-a-hay

               — these notes (bills)?
               — estos billetes?
               — es-tos bee-ye-tes

Here is my passport
Aquí tiene mi pasaporte
a-kee tee-e-nay mee pa-sa-por-tay

What is the rate of exchange?
¿A cuánto está el cambio?
a kwan-to es-ta el kam-bee-o

         What is the rate for — sterling?
   ¿A cuánto está el cambio — de la libra esterlina?
a kwan-to es-ta el kam-bee-o — day la lee-bra es-ter-lee-na

               — dollars?
               — del dólar?
               — del do-lar

What is your commission?
¿Cuánto es la comisión?
kwan-to es la ko-mee-syon

HEALTH

What's wrong?

I need a doctor
Necesito un médico
ne-the-see-to oon me-dee-ko

Can I see a doctor?
¿Puedo ver a un médico?
pwe-do bair a oon me-dee-ko

He is hurt
Está herido
es-ta e-ree-do

He has been badly injured
Está malherido
es-ta mal-e-ree-do

He has burnt himself
Él se ha quemado
el say a ke-ma-do

He has dislocated his shoulder
Él se ha dislocado el hombro
el say a dees-lo-ka-do el om-bro

He is unconscious
Está inconsciente
es-ta een-kons-thee-en-tay

She has a temperature
Ella tiene fiebre
e-ya tee-e-nay fee-e-bray

What's wrong?

She has been bitten
Ella tiene una mordedura
e-ya tee-e-nay oo-na mor-de-doo-ra

My son has cut himself
Mi hijo se ha hecho cortado
mee ee-ho say a e-cho kor-ta-do

My son is ill
Mi hijo está enfermo
mee ee-ho es-ta en-fair-mo

I am ill
Estoy enfermo
es-toy en-fair-mo

I am a diabetic
Soy diabético
soy dee-a-be-tee-ko

I am allergic to penicillin
Soy alérgico a la penicilina
soy a-lair-hee-ko a la pe-nee-thee-lee-na

I am badly sunburnt
Tengo quemaduras de sol
ten-go ke-ma-doo-ras day sol

I am constipated
Estoy estreñido
es-toy es-tren-yee-do

I cannot sleep
No puedo dormir
no pwe-do dor-meer

What's wrong?

I feel dizzy
Estoy mareado
es-toy ma-ray-a-do

I feel faint
Me siento mareado
may syen-to ma-ray-a-do

I feel nauseous
Siento náuseas
syen-to now-say-as

I fell
Me he caído
may ay ky-ee-do

I have a pain here
Me duele aquí
may dwe-lay a-kee

I have a rash here
Tengo un sarpullido aquí
ten-go oon sar-poo-yee-do a-kee

I have been sick
He estado vomitando
ay es-ta-do bo-mee-tan-do

I have been stung
Tengo una picadura
ten-go oo-na pee-ka-doo-ra

I have cut myself
Me he cortado
may ay kor-ta-do

What's wrong?

I have diarrhoea
Tengo diarrea
ten-go dee-a-ray-a

I have pulled a muscle
Tengo un tirón en un músculo
ten-go oon tee-ron en oon moo-skoo-lo

I have sunstroke
Tengo insolación
ten-go een-so-la-thyon

I suffer from high blood pressure
Tengo la tensión alta
ten-go la ten-syon al-ta

I think I have food poisoning
Creo que tengo una intoxicación de alimentos
kray-o kay ten-go oo-na een-tok-see-ka-thyon day a-lee-men-tos

It is inflamed here
Esto está inflamado
es-to es-ta een-fla-ma-do

My arm is broken
Me he roto el brazo
may ay ro-to el bra-tho

My stomach is upset
Tengo mal de estómago
ten-go mal day e-sto-ma-go

My tongue is coated
Tengo la lengua sucia
ten-go la len-gwa soo-thya

What's wrong?

There is a swelling here
Tengo hinchazón aquí
ten-go een-cha-thon a-kee

I have hurt — my arm
Me he hecho daño en — el brazo
may ay e-cho dan-yo en — el bra-tho

— my leg
— la pierna
— la pee-air-na

It is painful — to walk
Me duele al — caminar
may dwe-lay al — ka-mee-nar

— to breathe
— respirar
— re-spee-rar

— to swallow
— tragar
— tra-gar

I have — a headache
Tengo — dolor de cabeza
ten-go — do-lor day ka-bay-tha

— a sore throat
— dolor de garganta
— do-lor day gar-gan-ta

— an earache
— dolor de oído
— do-lor day oy-ee-do

What's wrong?

I am taking these drugs
Estoy tomando estos medicamentos
es-toy to-man-do es-tos me-dee-ka-men-tos

Can you give me a prescription for them?
¿Puede hacerme una receta para ellos?
pwe-day dar-may oo-na re-thay-ta pa-ra e-yos

I am on the pill
Estoy tomando la píldora
es-toy to-man-do la peel-do-ra

I am pregnant
Estoy embarazada
es-toy em-ba-ra-tha-da

My blood group is ...
Mi grupo sanguíneo es ...
mee groo-po san-gee-nay-o es ...

I do not know my blood group
No sé el grupo sanguíneo que tengo
no say el groo-po san-gee-nay-o kay ten-go

I need some antibiotics
Necesito antibióticos
ne-the-see-to an-tee-bee-o-tee-kos

Do I have to go into hospital?
¿Tengo que ir al hospital?
ten-go kay eer al o-spee-tal

Do I need an operation?
¿Tengo que operarme?
ten-go kay o-pe-rar-may

At the hospital

Here is my E-111 form
Aquí está mi formulario E-111 (ciento once)
a-kee es-ta mee for-moo-la-ree-o thee-en-to on-thay

How do I get reimbursed?
¿Cómo me van a reembolsar?
ko-mo may ban a ray-em-bol-sar

Must I stay in bed?
¿Tengo que estar en la cama?
ten-go kay es-tar en la ka-ma

When will I be able to travel?
¿Cuándo podré viajar?
kwan-do po-dray bee-a-har

Will I be able to go out tomorrow?
¿Podré salir mañana?
po-dray sa-leer man-ya-na

Parts of the body

ankle
tobillo
to-bee-yo

arm
brazo
bra-tho

back
espalda
es-pal-da

bone
hueso
we-so

Parts of the body

breast
pecho
pe-cho

cheek
mejilla
me-hee-ya

chest
pecho
pe-cho

ear
oreja
o-ray-ha

elbow
codo
ko-do

eye
ojo
o-ho

face
cara
ka-ra

finger
dedo
de-do

foot
pie
pee-ay

hand
mano
ma-no

heart
corazón
ko-ra-thon

kidney
riñon
reen-yon

knee
rodilla
ro-dee-ya

leg
pierna
pee-air-na

liver
hígado
ee-ga-do

lungs
pulmones
pool-mo-nes

mouth
boca
bo-ka

muscle
músculo
moos-koo-lo

Parts of the body

neck
cuello
kwe-yo

nose
nariz
na-reeth

skin
piel
pyel

stomach
estómago
e-sto-ma-go

throat
garganta
gar-gan-ta

wrist
muñeca
moon-yay-ka

At the dentist's

I have to see the dentist
Tengo que ir al dentista
ten-go kay eer al den-tee-sta

I have a toothache
Tengo dolor de muelas
ten-go do-lor day mway-las

Are you going to fill it?
¿Va a empastarme?
ba a em-pa-star-may

I have broken a tooth
Me ha roto una muela
may a ro-to oo-na mway-la

Will you have to take it out?
¿Tendrá que sacármela?
ten-dra kay sa-kar-may-la

At the dentist's

My false teeth are broken
Se me han roto los dientes postizos
*say may an **ro**-to los dee-**en**-tes po-**stee**-thos*

Can you repair them?
¿Puede reparármelos?
*pwe-day re-pa-**rar**-may-los*

My gums are sore
Me duelen las encías
*may **dwe**-len las en-**thee**-as*

Please give me an injection
Póngame una inyección, por favor
*pon-ga-may **oo**-na een-yek-**thyon**, por fa-**bor***

That hurts
Eso duele
*e-so **dwe**-lay*

The filling has come out
Se me ha caído el empaste
*say may a ky-ee-do el em-**pas**-tay*

This one hurts
Me duele ésta
*may **dwe**-lay es-ta*

FOR YOUR INFORMATION

Numbers

0	cero	*the-ro*
1	uno	*oo-no*
2	dos	*dos*
3	tres	*tres*
4	cuatro	*kwa-tro*
5	cinco	*theen-ko*
6	seis	*says*
7	siete	*see-e-tay*
8	ocho	*o-cho*
9	nueve	*nwe-bay*
10	diez	*dee-eth*
11	once	*on-thay*
12	doce	*do-thay*
13	trece	*tre-thay*
14	catorce	*ka-tor-thay*
15	quince	*keen-thay*
16	dieciséis	*dee-eth-ee-says*
17	diecisiete	*dee-eth-ee-see-e-tay*
18	dieciocho	*dee-eth-ee-o-cho*

Numbers

19	diecinueve	*dee-eth-ee-**nwe**-bay*
20	veinte	***bain**-tay*
21	veintiuno	*bain-tee-**oo**-no*
22	veintidós	*bain-tee-**dos***
23	veintitrés	*bain-tee-**tres***
24	veinticuatro	*bain-tee-**kwa**-tro*
25	veinticinco	*bain-tee-**theen**-ko*
26	veintiséis	*bain-tee-**says***
27	veintisiete	*bain-tee-see-**e**-tay*
28	veintiocho	*bain-tee-**o**-cho*
29	veintinueve	*bain-tee-**nwe**-bay*
30	treinta	***trayn**-ta*
40	cuarenta	*kwa-**ren**-ta*
50	cincuenta	*theen-**kwen**-ta*
60	sesenta	*se-**sen**-ta*
70	setenta	*se-**ten**-ta*
80	ochenta	*o-**chen**-ta*
90	noventa	*no-**ben**-ta*
100	cien, ciento	*thee-**en**, thee-**en**-to*
200	doscientos	*dos-thee-**en**-tos*
300	trescientos	*tres-thee-**en**-tos*

Numbers

400	cuatrocientos	*kwa-tro-thee-en-tos*
500	quinientos	*keen-yen-tos*
600	seiscientos	*says-thee-en-tos*
700	setecientos	*se-tay-thee-en-tos*
800	ochocientos	*o-cho-thee-en-tos*
900	novecientos	*no-bay-thee-en-tos*
1000	mil	*meel*
2000	dos mil	*dos meel*
3000	tres mil	*tres meel*
4000	cuatro mil	*kwa-tro meel*
1000000	un millón	*oon mee-yon*

Ordinals

1st	primero	*pree-**mair**-o*
2nd	segundo	*se-**goon**-do*
3rd	tercero	*tair-**thair**-o*
4th	cuarto	*kwar-to*
5th	quinto	*keen-to*
nth	enésimo	*e-ne-see-mo*

Fractions and percentages

a half	medio *me-dee-o*
a quarter	un cuarto *oon kwar-to*
a third	un tercio *oon tair-thee-o*
two thirds	dos tercios *dos tair-thee-os*
10 %	diez por ciento *dee-eth por thee-en-to*

Days

Sunday	domingo *do-meen-go*
Monday	lunes *loo-nes*
Tuesday	martes *mar-tes*
Wednesday	miércoles *mee-air-ko-les*
Thursday	jueves *hwe-bes*
Friday	viernes *bee-air-nes*
Saturday	sábado *sa-ba-do*

Dates

on Friday	el viernes *el bee-air-nes*
next Tuesday	el martes próximo *el mar-tes prok-see-mo*
last Tuesday	el martes pasado *el mar-tes pa-sa-do*
yesterday	ayer *a-yair*
today	hoy *oy*
tomorrow	mañana *man-ya-na*
in June	en junio *en hoo-nee-o*
July 7th	el siete de julio *el see-e-tay day hoo-lee-o*
next week	la semana que viene *la se-ma-na kay bee-e-nay*
last month	el mes pasado *el mes pa-sa-do*

The seasons

spring	primavera *pree-ma-bair-a*
summer	verano *be-ra-no*
autumn	otoño *o-ton-yo*
winter	invierno *een-byair-no*

Times of the year

in spring	en la primavera *en la pree-ma-bair-a*
in summer	en el verano *en el be-ra-no*
in autumn	en el otoño *en el o-ton-yo*
in winter	en el invierno *en el een-byair-no*

Months

January	enero *e-nair-o*
February	febrero *fe-brair-o*
March	marzo *mar-tho*
April	abril *a-breel*
May	mayo *my-o*
June	junio *hoo-nee-o*
July	julio *hoo-lee-o*
August	agosto *a-go-sto*
September	setiembre *se-tee-em-bray*
October	octubre *ok-too-bray*
November	noviembre *nob-yem-bray*
December	diciembre *deeth-yem-bray*

Public holidays

Public holidays

January 1, New Year's Day
Año Nuevo
an-yo nway-bo

January 6, Epiphany
Día de Reyes
dee-a day ray-es

19 March, St Joseph's Day
San José
san ho-say

Holy Thursday
Jueves Santo
hwe-bes san-to

Good Friday
Viernes Santo
bee-air-nes san-to

Easter Monday
Lunes de Pascua
loo-nes day pas-kwa

May 1, May Day
Día del Trabajo
dee-a del tra-ba-ho

Corpus Christi Day
Corpus Christi
kor-poos kree-stee

Public holidays

25 July, St James's Day
Santiago Apóstol
san-tya-go a-po-stol

15 August, Assumption
Asunción
a-soon-thyon

12 October, Columbus Day
Día del Virgin del Pilar
dee-a del beer-hen del pee-lar

1 November, All Saints Day
Todos los Santos
to-dos los san-tos

6 December, Constitution Day
Día de la Constitución
dee-a day la kon-stee-too-thyon

8 December, Immaculate Conception
Inmaculada Concepción
een-ma-koo-la-da kon-thep-thyon

25 December, Christmas Day
Navidad
na-bee-dad

Colours

Colours

black
negro
ne-gro

blue
azul
a-thool

brown
marrón
ma-ron

cream
crema
kray-ma

fawn
beis
bays

gold
dorado
do-ra-do

green
verde
bair-day

grey
gris
grees

orange
naranja
na-ran-ha

pink
rosa
ro-sa

purple
morado
mo-ra-do

red
rojo
ro-ho

silver
plateado
pla-tay-a-do

tan
color canela
ko-lor ka-nay-la

white
blanco
blan-ko

yellow
amarillo
a-ma-ree-yo

Common adjectives

bad
malo
ma-lo

beautiful
hermoso
air-mo-so

big
grande
gran-day

cheap
barato
ba-ra-to

cold
frío
free-o

expensive
caro
ka-ro

difficult
difícil
dee-fee-theel

easy
fácil
fa-theel

fast
rápido
ra-pee-do

good
bueno
bway-no

high
alto
al-to

hot
caliente
ka-lee-en-tay

little
poco
po-ko

long
largo
lar-go

new
nuevo
nway-bo

old
viejo
bee-ay-ho

Common adjectives

short
corto
kor-to

small
pequeño
pe-ken-yo

slow
lento
len-to

ugly
feo
fay-o

Signs and notices

cuidado
caution
kwee-da-do

ascensor
lift/elevator
as-then-sor

salida
exit
sa-lee-da

información
information
een-for-ma-thyon

abierto
open
a-bee-air-to

llame
ring
ya-may

rebajas
sale
re-ba-has

agotado
sold out
a-go-ta-do

ocupado
occupied
o-koo-pa-do

no pisar el césped
keep off the grass
no pee-sar el thes-ped

llame por favor
please ring
ya-may por fa-bor

empujar
push
em-poo-har

entrada
entrance
en-tra-da

entre sin llamar
enter without knocking
en-tray seen ya-mar

entrada gratuita
no admission charge
en-tra-da gra-twee-ta

prohibido hacer fotos
no picture taking
pro-ee-bee-do a-thair fo-tos

Signs and notices

teléfono
telephone
te-le-fo-no

prohibida la entrada
No trespassing
pro-ee-bee-da la en-tra-da

bomberos
fire brigade
bom-bair-os

peligro
danger
pe-lee-gro

libre
vacant
lee-bray

cerrado
closed
the-ra-do

llegadas
arrivals
ye-ga-das

veneno
poison
be-nay-no

colegio
school
co-le-hee-o

caliente
hot
ka-lee-en-tay

entrada
entrance
en-tra-da

frío
cold
free-o

horario
timetable
o-ra-ree-o

cajero
cashier
ka-hair-o

caballeros
gentlemen
ka-ba-yair-os

prohibido el paso
no thoroughfare
pro-ee-bee-do el pa-so

señoras
ladies
sen-yo-ras

no entrar
no entry
no en-trar

Signs and notices

hospital
hospital
os-pee-tal

ambulancia
ambulance
am-boo-lan-thee-a

peligro de muerte
danger of death
pe-lee-gro day mwair-tay

cerrado por la tarde
closed in the afternoon
the-ra-do por la tar-day

no tocar
do not touch
no to-kar

prohibido fumar
no smoking
pro-ee-bee-do foo-ma

timbre de alarma
communication cord
teem-bray day a-lar-ma

camino particular
private road
ka-mee-no par-tee-koo-lar

carril de bicicleta
cycle path
ka-reel day bee-thee-klay-ta

venta de liquidación
closing down sale
ben-ta day lee-kee-da-thyon

recuerdos
souvenirs
re-kwair-dos

agencia de viajes
travel agency
a-hen-thee-a day bee-a-hes

oferta especial
special offer
o-fair-ta es-peth-yal

agua potable
drinking water
a-gwa po-ta-blay

baggage
equipaje
e-kee-pa-hay

bank
banco
ban-ko

Customs
aduana
a-dwa-na

emergency
emergencia
e-mair-hen-thee-a

Signs and notices

fire alarm
alarma de incendios
a-lar-ma day een-then-dee-os

bienvenido
welcome
byen-be-nee-do

police
policía
po-lee-thee-a

permitido sólo para...
allowed only for...
pair-mee-tee-do so-lo pa-ra...

reserved
reservado
re-sair-ba-do

cuidado con el perro
beware of the dog
kwee-da-do kon el pe-ro

smoking area
área de fumadores
a-ray-a day foo-ma-do-res

policía
police
po-lee-thee-a

desviación
diversion
des-bee-a-thyon

peligro de incendio
danger of fire
pe-lee-gro day een-then-dee-o

tirar
pull
tee-rar

sólo empleados
employees only
so-lo em-play-a-dos

se vende
for sale
say ben-day

salidas
departures
sa-lee-das

se alquila
to let/for hire
say al-kee-la

prohibido asomarse
do not lean out
pro-ee-bee-do a-so-mar-say

lista de precios
price list
lee-sta day pre-thee-os

papelera
litter
pa-pe-lair-a

Signs and notices

sólo para uso externo
for external use only
so-lo pa-ra oo-so ek-stair-no

compartimento de fumadores
smoking compartment
kom-par-tee-men-to day foo-ma-do-res

está prohibido hablar al conductor mientras circula
It is forbidden to speak to the driver while the bus is
moving
*es-ta pro-ee-bee-do a-blar kon el kon-dook-tor myen-tras
theer-koo-la*

Oficina de objetos perdidos
Lost property office
o-fee-thee-na day ob-he-tos pair-dee-dos

aparcamiento sólo para residentes
parking for residents only
a-par-ka-myen-to so-lo pa-ra re-see-den-tes

circule por la derecha
keep to the right
theer-koo-lay por la de-ray-cha

salida de emergencia
emergency exit
sa-lee-da day e-mair-hen-thee-a

In an Emergency

Call — the fire brigade
Llame — a los bomberos
*ya-may — a los bom-**bair**-os*

— the police
— a la policía
*— a la po-lee-**thee**-a*

—an ambulance
— a una ambulancia
*— a **oo**-na am-boo-**lan**-thee-a*

Get a doctor
Busque a un médico
***boos**-kay a oon **me**-dee-ko*

There is a fire
Hay un incendio
*a-ee oon en-**then**-dee-o*

Where is — the British consulate?
¿Dónde está — el consulado británico?
***don**-day es-**ta** — el kon-soo-**la**-do bree-**ta**-nee-ko*

— the police station?
— la comisaría de policía?
*— la ko-mee-sa-**ree**-a day po-lee-**thee**-a*